HOW TO NURTURE
TRUTH AND AUTHENTICITY

A Metamodern Economic Reform Proposal

JUSTIN CARMIEN

978-0-6452126-7-9
How to Nurture Truth and Authenticity:
A Metamodern Economic Reform Proposal
Justin Carmien

Edited by Adam James Davis

Artwork by Matt Betteker

Thema Classification: KCA (Economic Theory & Philosophy), QDTS (Social & Political Philosophy), QDX (Popular Philosophy).

MANTICORE PRESS
WWW.MANTICORE.PRESS

CONTENTS

FIRST HALF DIVISIONS

01. Truth in a Time Between Worlds 7

02. The Historical Movement of Truth 29

03. *Αληθεια, Verum*, Truth 41

04. Epistemology, the Metaphysics of Colonialism 53

05. Fallen Empires 69

06. The Liberal Solution, Metamodernism 83

SECOND HALF DIVISIONS

07. Truth for an Emergent Project 99

08. *Αληθευειν*, Foundation for a New Economy 111

09. The Encounter as the Venue for Truth 127

10. *Δημιουργος* and the Proximity of *Αληθευειν* 135

11. *Societas* as the Barometer of Truth 153

12. Drawing New Definitions for Governance 169

13. Localizing the Horizons of Projection 189

14. Closing Exercise with Three Pictures 205

15. Objections to the Proposal 213

Annotated Bibliography 229
Glossary of Key Terms 261
About the Author 269

FIRST HALF

Truth in a Time Between Worlds

Orgasmic. Sensual. Ecstatic. This is the experience of truth. For our ancestors, the phenomena which produced such sensual experience was appreciated. Ultimately, our progenitors felt indebted, and in reflection, they revered the sensual experience—they drew temporal and spatial definition, capturing it in name: *the beautiful, the good,* and *the just.* The human soul could hardly be felt as responsible for such creation, and in these times the meditations of kings led to expressions of humility. In reading these meditations today, we transport ourselves by way of a silent profundity—we experience their words as a deaf man might feel the resonance of the trumpet's blast,

> "Beautiful things are beautiful in themselves and sufficient to themselves. Praise is extraneous."

> "Does anything genuinely beautiful need supplementing? No more than justice does—or truth, or kindness, or humility. Are any of those improved by being praised? Or damaged by contempt?"

> "Is an emerald suddenly flawed if no one admires it?"

These passages come to us by way of a translation of Marcus Aurelius' diary-like meditations by Martin Hammond.

But let us stop for just a moment. With all fairness to yourself and the Roman emperor, try asking yourself this, *how uncanny did these reflections strike you*? In all honesty, wasn't a certain degree of dissociation required for appreciating their profundity? I mean, wouldn't you be embarrassed to express the sentiments of the emperor as your own, today? Imagine if a friend was standing right in front of you. Right now. How do you anticipate this friend's reaction? Would you not expect laughter? Would you not be accused of speaking absurdities? *"Beautiful things are beautiful in themselves"*—seriously?

Today, the poets and kings, along with the ancient philosophers, are understood as harboring a self-absorbed naivety towards the world. There is nothing novel in admitting that long ago we lost the privilege to express such praise for the world. Such sensual experience, it is said, is the least likely thing that could be called "objective". Today, we are of such a maturity that we admit suspicion towards flattering these experiences. Each one of us are kings—or perhaps if you prefer, none of us. And actually, neither the elevation nor degradation of our position matters; the consequence *here* is the same. The experience which calls us to proclaim *the beautiful*, *the good*, and *the just* have fallen into doubt. Today, we feel that the Roman emperor's sensual experience wants to burst forth from inside us—we want to say that *that which is beautiful to me is also beautiful in itself,* but our conscience prevents us from expressing it, outside of art museum "safe spaces", at least. No doubt, we are all too wise. After all, who today could comfort themselves with the thought of possessing something like *my* truths. The very expression feels like a contradiction. Either my experience is true for everyone, or it is nothing even to myself.

Looking back within history, we can theme a narrative of our social and material inheritance—a project which we have called *modernization*. Within this story, we find a demand for institutions where the truth of matters could be decided. Beyond the courtroom this project demanded that the decisions be given over to investigators—the physicians and journalists. Inasmuch, the judgement to discern truth was industrialized. We had undertaken the quest for a compendium of knowledge for the sake of human liberation—and only those procedures which facilitated this industrial-liberation project enjoyed our praise as *the good*. And yet, for those of you who hold this work before you, one thing must be certain—that you have felt an unsatisfactory commitment towards truth. Only on account of this dissatisfaction can a work which is titled *How to Nurture Truth and Authenticity* spark any interest. Therefore, this work assumes an atomic dissonance. A feeling that, in some way, we have not done a satisfactory job of nurturing the disclosure of truth within this economy. Of course, our dissonance is founded upon real examples. Yet, we cannot surmise *here* those cases which you, the reader, bring to this work. Despite this, we can say that during the period of later modernization we seem to have harbored an almost universal suspicion towards government officials and those lobbying on behalf of capital interests. This distrust is apparent in the appeal which populist rhetoric entertained on both sides of the political spectrum: both Left and Right. However, we should not be too quick to point fingers. After all, an example can also be made of our equally pervasive encouragement of self-concealment. Insofar as truth not only contains industrial information (factual data)—but also reports on our subjective states (for example, pain, hoping, or grieving), and those of aesthetic description (beautiful, good, just, exotic, or uncanny)—we can say that we have encouraged something of a reservation towards disclosure in general. Undoubtedly, we have all heard the disclaimer, *we don't talk politics or religion at the dinner table.* Of course, when looking at family economy during this period of later modernization, we can understand the necessity of this disclaimer. However, we can also understand the necessity as evidence of an unsatisfactory interpersonal commerce. After all, wouldn't any professional psychologist warn against such reservation? Such lonesome suffering with *your* truth? It should not be any surprise that many had found solace within the internet echo chamber. Alternative infrastructure manifested to cope with symptoms resulting from the existing democratic platforms. No doubt, pronounced for us today is the understanding that the democratic ideal is not merely satisfied by the vote, but by the larger civic commerce which precludes the vote—whether that be engagement at the family dinner table or in the publicness of the internet news journal. Of course, it goes without saying that the disclosure of *the good, the just,* and *the true* are of primary importance to satisfying this ideal. Therefore, we conclude, it is that we harbor the democratic ideal, today, that we suffer from a dissatisfaction with the disclosure of truth.

Now, while the family dinner table may be a very relatable example, it is perhaps our virtue of privacy which best exemplifies the encouragement of self-concealment. After all, while privacy is self-evidently healthy, we must also admit that it is a symptom—one which is highly encouraged within a commodification of information. Yet, while this may be true, all the same, raising such a self-evident virtue into question provokes suspicion of our agenda—or at the very least, what conclusions a project concerning itself with nurturing truth and authenticity might reach. We want to ask, *what exactly are we committing ourselves to in interrogating our dissatisfaction with the disclosure of truth?* This is a question not to be shunned aside. It is required of us already now, here at the outset of this opuscule.

Evidently, the first hesitation which presents itself might be called *death from exposure*. After all, if we were to act upon our dissatisfaction with the disclosure of truth, and thereby nurture conditions for *more disclosure*, we might end up on the edge of a slippery slope. What if we find ourselves butt naked, exposed and without even leaves to cover ourselves back up? Of course, here we should also remind ourselves that conditions do exist in which something like a "healthy lie" has value. No doubt, we must remember that there are times in which concealment is appropriate. Therefore, if we choose to investigate our dissatisfaction, and thereby advance towards prescriptions for nurturing the disclosure of truth, we should not fear that we are likewise interested in depriving the individual of their right to discretion in their day-to-day encounters. On the contrary, if we choose to investigate our dissatisfaction further, then it is only for the sake of a liberation *for* disclosure.

Secondly, we can be sure that any prescriptions for nurturing the disclosure of truth could not take the form of self-help. Obviously, nurturing a readiness for disclosure in any particular *you* or *me* would surely be disadvantageous for anyone whose environment did not mutually support such disclosure. And neither can anything interesting come in faulting any individual for the discouragement of disclosure anyway. Consider that there is nothing particularly novel in critiquing capitalism on the basis of greed or selfishness. Likewise, nothing interesting can come from looking at dissimulation, deception, and concealment as deviations from normal behavior from within our inherited infrastructure. Inasmuch, we understand that any deception, dissimulation, or concealment of the truth has only surfaced as a by-product of our interpersonal commerce. We should beware of becoming preoccupied with policing deviant cases and domesticating the human animal. Of course, both shame and virtue signaling have been employed in appeals to the modern ideal of society. The persistence of woke narrative throughout the early third millennium indicates the popularity of the "armchair sociologist". And today, offerings are still made to appease this god, *Society* (—such that it demands a capital "S"!) Yet, if we wish to take up a project interested in nurturing the disclosure of truth, we must admit that nothing interesting can come from such a domestication of the human animal. Nurturing the disclosure of truth means precisely the opposite—a *liberation* for disclosure. Furthermore, "domestication" can only derail us from the more fruitful tasks which come from understanding that our infrastructure is currently providing for operations well in accordance with its principles. In other words, we understand that truth is doing what it should be doing. Therefore, the form of our conclusions must be clear. We are not interested in self-help, nor are we interested in social conditioning, but rather in economic reform—and this means that we are interested in reforming the ways in which we encounter each other and the whole of nature, by way of our everyday commerce.

Should we be convinced, then, that these preliminary precautions have prepared us for initiating an investigation into our dissatisfaction with the disclosure of truth? Hardly. We can also admit to a third hesitation. After all, there is a serious question concerning practicality. Obviously, we have a limited number of resources at hand at any given moment, and pursuing economic reform of this type may mean sacrificing other projects. Therefore, a requirement for such a project is the estimation of its value. Of course, understanding its value means understanding firstly the challenge, but also the outcome. Therefore, as we think about such an estimation, we must ask ourselves in all honesty, *why do we harbor such dissatisfaction towards the disclosure of truth?* Is our dissatisfaction a mere symptom? The answer to that is most likely going to be "yes". If so, are we then aiming at an outcome other than simply *more truth?*

We have already identified the ideal of democracy as the source of our dissatisfaction, and we have already admitted that democracy, for us today, cannot merely maintain through the institutions of value measurement. And in a perfect democracy, no vote would be necessary anyway— we would simply follow our government's administrators, who would, after all, be each and every one of us. Democracy, as *a rule of the people,* is the form of governance which is produced from *the national ideal.* However, insofar as we are far from *this* democracy, we do assume each mark on the ballot as a token of truth; yet, we also acknowledge that democracy is maintained by the larger civic commerce which precludes such value measurement. The word *democracy* refers us to that which produces a sense of the truth, such that only subsequently, value can be measured and maintained by way of democratic institutions. However, in animating *"that which produces a sense of truth",* we are not thereby also interested in the mob rule of social domestication; we have already made this much clear. Therefore, when investigating our dissatisfaction with the disclosure of truth—as an obstacle to the ideal of democracy—then *the conditions for authenticity* are that which draw forward as our fundamental aim. Those conditions announce themselves negatively, in moments when authenticity has been barred. We find testament to such barring by looking into the history of later modernization.

Looking through the story of industrial-liberation, we find references to what has been called *alienation*. Testimony of this experience can be found going at least as far back as the Bohemian novelist Franz Kafka. But looking even further back, the Scottish economist Adam Smith had already recognized an alienation of the worker from his labor in *the division of labor*. We can furthermore turn towards communist literature. If we do, and if we allow ourselves to sympathize with the reasons why communist economy was even explored in the first place, we then find language for refining the description of Smith's *"division"*. According to Karl Marx, the industrial worker loses the ability to determine both life and destiny when deprived of the right to: firstly, think of himself as the director of his own actions; or secondly, to determine the character of his actions; or thirdly, to own the items of value produced by his own labor, and so on. Finding himself at the lower stratification of the social classes, the industrial worker is subordinated to the bourgeoisie—much like the Hebrew to the Pharaoh. Of course, today, and after looking back to this period of industrial development, we can surmise that the symptoms described by alienation must not have been merely an illness for those employed on the assembly line, or of the proletariat class. Instead, these symptoms must have been conditioned by something much more pervasive—a condition which points towards a more atomic dissatisfaction with the disclosure of truth.

From the higher vantage point afforded to us today, we can understand industrialization as referring to the specialization and compartmentalization of system operations, generally. If we consider the "system operation" of an individual's perpetual interpretation of the sensual experience, then it seems that the very digestion of the world, as we experience it through industry journals and other news media, had given cause for a certain alienation. This source of alienation is evidenced in the many critiques we hear waged against that form of governance which has been called *technocracy*—a form of governance in which industry specialists contribute to the "world picture" by way of various public touchpoints. Further evidence of this alienation can be found in the attempted answers to technocratic governance. For example, today, we find that the self-help industry has been supplanted with what has been called a *meaning- and sense-making* industry. This industry is composed of YouTube and other social media "gurus" who provide relief to their audience by digesting the various public touchpoints, from specialists and non-specialists alike, across both television broadcast and social media, into digestible world-encompassing *grand narratives*. Given this evidence, we may want to venture an explanation. If we do, then we might diagnose, as a cause of this alienation, the deprivation in the individual agent's affectivity in the process of creating the world image. This explanation would also allow us to understand the rise and belief in conspiracy theories— namely, as a result of anxieties caused by this deprivation. However, and despite this seemingly recent development, what should not be overlooked is that early in the twentieth century, during the period of the German Conservative Revolution, this form of alienation had already been identified. In the words of the interpreters and translators of this period, we read of a *rootlessness*—an estrangement from that which is produced in the proximity of the workshop, through trades, guilds, apprenticeships, and characterized as being *of the people and of the land.* This period of writing produced a romanticized picture of the ancients—a picture which we can still find resonating within ourselves, even today. We only need to consider the thousands of years of conditioning which the human animal must have adjusted for during the polytheistic agricultural period—a time we imagine as being characterized by a harmonious feedback loop between labor and the proximal phenomenal experience. Of course, today, rootlessness may seem like a mere self-diagnosis and battle cry for the ethnonationalists. Yet, we turn towards this period of German conservatism in order to borrow more language for further identifying our dissatisfaction with the disclosure of truth as an obstacle to the ideal of democracy. And, after all, it seems that neither are "democracy-loving Americans" exempt from this particular experience of alienation. For example, if we read the work of American social critic Walter Lippmann as testimony from the same period (that which has been said to have introduced the world to modern journalism) and the contemporaneous American philosopher John Dewey, then we find contentions with an impersonal *public.* This public was a *you* and a *me,* yet at the same time, it was a *no one.* And what should not be contested is the consequence of such an impersonal object—a coddled people. It seems that the liberated had become, quite perversely, sheltered from one another by way of the public—or rather, by way of the world image held by *this no one in particular.* It seems that without the necessary fora for sincere and meaningful encounters, truth had been stripped from the human mouth. The modern state was a nation without a campfire, so to speak. And if we consider the effect of this void—if we are to be truly honest with ourselves—then we must admit that the modern state had encouraged a harmful appeal to the distances and differences between its people—a *"pathos of distance"* (Friedrich Nietzsche). Undoubtedly, the liberated had come to enjoy the fiction of the misguided stranger—that individual who is responsible for electing the corrupted politicians and the self-defeating legislation. However, today, we are too mature for such a characterization. Instead, we must admit that any failure of democracy can only be an indication of an unhealthy economy—an indication of an unhealthy *democracy of strangers*. Undoubtedly, the source of this form of alienation (which we might diagnose as an *estrangement* from one another) is attested for in the cool-aloofness, or sarcastic-cynicism, of late-twentieth-century popular culture. Any one of us can recall our sympathy for the apathetic characters of Donn Pearce's *Cool Hand Luke* and Marshall Mathers' Eminem. Therefore, it seems that the very product of modernization—the super-sized modern empire—had marginalized not only the indigenous cultures, but also the individuals comprising majority demographics as well.

It is only from these long-told stories of alienation, rootlessness, estrangement, and apathy that we understand the direness of our dissatisfaction with the disclosure of truth. No doubt, the want for authenticity proves itself, still today, in the failure of the democratic institution of independent news media—when "post-truth!" announces itself. Perhaps the want for authenticity proves itself less explicitly in the *"utilitarian state"* (Étienne Balibar) subjected to market demands—but even so, it proves itself once again, and more pronounced, in the mob contagion of social justice activism which produces content for abuse by marketeers. This is no light matter. After all, we can ask ourselves, *how can any one of us retain genuine authenticity when the social and material condition calls for unprecedented unity?* Estrangement is pronounced in the revenge of the post-colonial narratives and political activism; it is equally pronounced in the reactionary masculinist movements (Jack Donovan, *et al*), and in calls for the founding of ethnostates. We are pitted against each other—neighbor against neighbor, friend against friend, and relative against relative. Can there be any doubt that such a state of affairs obscures the possibility for genuine authenticity?

But what signals that *today* we have a position adequate for going beyond these long-told symptoms? Why this opuscule? Why exactly today? No doubt, alienation, rootlessness, estrangement, and apathy are nothing new to industrialized economies. So, what is it that we have now which previous economists lacked? Authenticity was, after all, championed during the twentieth century in the works of the German philosopher Martin Heidegger and psychologist Karl Jaspers. The search for authenticity has been attributed to what has been called the existentialist period of Western philosophy. And yet, that body of work fell to critique by way of Theodor Adorno, who argued that the material economy of the human animal precludes *"the divine right of the soul"*. That is, the material condition of the human body is that which conditions the movements of the human soul. Material first. Soul second. Therefore, Adorno suggests, we must prioritize the material condition over the liberation of authenticity.

Inasmuch, it seems that our task is this: *are we able to do today what was not possible in the post-WWII liberal witch-hunt?*—during the time of the Frankfurt School's critical theory. Can we bring authenticity to meet economic reform? Of course, in order to do this, it appears that we must make a decision about what is more foundational—the soul of "man", or the body. In his essay, *The Jargon of Authenticity*, Adorno is clear: the *"states of affairs"* is that which *"precludes the divine rights of the soul"*. But, in making such a decision about Adorno's *"man"*, we must remember that when Marx *stood Hegel on his head* in order to announce dialectical materialism, we *were* delivered over to a certain truth—but this was not that the movement of the human soul is conditioned by a material substrate. Instead, the human soul is moved by an *appeal* to our material conditioning: soul first, material second. Let us remember even Marx's own primordial movement of the soul: the pains of alienation. Inasmuch, we return to Marx's soul, not his predictions of a proletariat revolution. In doing so, we realize that a starting point in material economics is exactly that which has prevented an overcoming of alienation, rootlessness, estrangement, and apathy. Certainly, economics as a dialectic—that is, between classes, races, genders, or whatever other identities have followed from material dialectics—are narrow and divisive. What an investigation into our dissatisfaction requires is a new position from which to view economics. Let us make this much clear— this opuscule, if it is to be satisfactory, cannot deliver a *mere* social or material economic proposal, but rather something which renders an appeal to such material economics possible. We must operate within the sphere of a more *primordial economics*—one which operates parallel to Aristotle's metaphysics, τα περι της πρωτης φιλοσοφιας (that is, "the [writings] concerning **first philosophy**"). The French philosopher Rene Descartes offers a more English-friendly term for this realm of thought: *prima philosophia*. And so, following the Latinized expression, we might say that we are here doing *prima* economics: prime economics. However, for ease of translation into English, let us simply name the realm in which this opuscule operates: *first economics.*

On account of our position, ready to make real prescriptions for nurturing truth and authenticity (as well as for going beyond the illnesses of industrialized economy), we also acknowledge that, today, we are living in a *"time between worlds"*—a phrase which has become popular through American education philosopher Zak Stein. Of course, it is yet to be known whether the liminal *here* and *now* referenced throughout this work will span decades or centuries. However, and despite this uncertainty, there is one thought which should inspire confidence in our future. Consider that you are already here with this work. Together, we are actively seeking a vision which can align our activities. Thus, we are already building something of a coalition as we press ahead wide-eyed into the next world-defining project. If we look at both truth and authenticity as something of a seed, then their future is alone in our hands. If we wish to nurture them, then we must provide the conditions for them to grow—such that one day we can enjoy their blossom.

Structure of Our Argument and of the Delivery of Our Prescription

This work, *How to Nurture Truth and Authenticity*, will be delivered in two halves. The first seeks to disclose the historical economy of truth. This is in order to discover the cause of a deprivation of the phenomenal experience of truth. In recounting this narrative backwards through the Western historical continuum, we will lay bare an understanding of Ancient Greek αληθεια (*alētheia*, "truth") and the appropriation which overcame αληθεια through Latinization (into *verum*). In doing so, we anticipate the discovery of a moment of pronounced expediency in the project of modernization. This work will make clear the wholesale expediency of modernization by way of esteem for Latin *ratio* ("reason"). This narrative will also provide us with language for thematizing a specific comportment which made use of that expedient. In order that we may operate with this comportment as an object, this work will name this comportment with a word—*episteme*. The identification of episteme will itself allow for an understanding of the reification of the explanatory object *power*. The identification of these two-fold complimentary objects will allow us to frame the utility which truth assumed in the project of later modernization, in service to *imperium* ("command"). This utility will lay bare the deprivation of truth in later modernization. The identification of this deprivation will also affirm the necessity of a work concerning itself with truth and authenticity. In the second half of this opuscule, the reader should expect the delineation of a more robust understanding of truth. This delineation will be accomplished by way of an architectonic of truth. This architectonic will be used for identifying the economic conditions for the phenomenal encounter with truth—that which is itself the condition for authenticity. This architectonic will be constructed using the tools which are on offer here, courtesy of the discipline which is studied under the name *metaphysics*. Of course, as is well known, the two philosophers regarded as the premier metaphysicians of the modern era are Immanuel Kant and Martin Heidegger. Kant sought a description of the conditions for experience—"internal" time and "external" space, for example. Those conditions allow for the world *to be known*. Contrarily, Heidegger sought the conditions for the world *to be*. Both schools of metaphysical understanding follow from Aristotle, and they regard a category of objects which belong to a description of *the conditions of possibility*. This type of description has also been called "transcendental". If we take the meaning of transcendental explanation to be that which describes the conditions of possibility for *the world to be* (and not merely the conditions of possibility for *experience*), then our architectonic too can be said to belong to the tradition of transcendentalism. However, we should be careful with this self-identification. This is on account of the popular meaning of "transcendence", especially in theological circles. For us, "transcendental" cannot refer to that relationship which exists between the human animal's "inner experience" and that which is beyond it. Such theological distinctions, if directed at metaphysics as a critique, are dated. They could only correctly critique the state of metaphysics following Kant's *Kritik der reinen Vernunft* (*Critique of Pure Reason*). However, and to be sure, the discipline of metaphysics has progressed. We can assume that Heidegger has already dissolved the theological distinction between transcendental and immanent philosophy some time ago. Of course, in order to be clear, it must also be said that this word *metaphysics* has also been used to refer to another category of objects—namely, those objects which fall outside the possibility of physical description, yet are in some causal relationship with the objects of the physical world. This category of objects can be exemplified by *luck, destiny, will,* or even *social power and economic competition.* And while these objects may be helpful in explaining historical events, we can call this category *occult*, borrowing language from the translators of the Austrian philosopher, Ludwig Wittgenstein. It should be further noted that at times throughout this opuscule, it will be necessary to designate certain objects as belonging to this second category. Therefore, for clarity and emphasis, we will call this second category of objects *causal-occult*. Finally, once this architectonic has been established, we can then proceed to our prescriptions for material economic reform. Our prescriptions will be delivered using an enumerated list of the reform's features. These features will then be complimented with a guide for their interpretation, and also, with guidance for maintaining the intention behind these prescriptions.

While this work has been constructed under the presumption that Enlightenment values will continue to guide every project in our futural continuum, this work will also diagnose a perversion of those values—namely, that approach to governance which has gone by the name *liberalism*. No doubt, this claim may be shocking to those who champion the universal ideal of human rights. However, we can also be sure that liberal values (even those of which Marx made an appeal) have not delivered us over to a satisfactory commitment to truth. And unless we are interested in a domestication of the human animal—a quite *unliberal* project—these values must come under scrutiny. For those who are acquainted with the metamodern discussion, we must alay concern for what has been called *the problematizing of critique* from within the liberal paradigm. In deflating this concern, our prescriptions will have addressed the challenges of later modernization—namely, alienation, rootlessness, estrangement, and apathy. In the second half of this opuscule we will overcome the relativism which results from liberating individuals, each into their own lonesome worlds, and return truth to its rightful place in nature. Of course, it should be innately intuitive that a people who are attuned to a liberation of authenticity are those who are actively nurturing the conditions for healthy civic engagement—that which can satisfy our ideal of democracy. We understand that a liberation of authenticity can only be achieved by way of intimacy and listening, safety and security, sympathy and understanding. Inasmuch, the prescriptions herein offer better solutions for liberty than what liberalism can offer to us today.

Despite the dramatic claims contained within this introduction, it should be remarked that this opuscule does not harbor the spirit of revolutionary destruction. This opuscule is not a piece of futurism in which its own history has been erased. Of course, philosophers and social critics are often criticized for wanting to start over—for wanting to scrap the perverted infrastructure which we have inherited and begin afresh. After all, without that baggage, it is easy to visualize a utopia. However, this is likely a misconception. Certainly, this opuscule would be fooling its reader if it entertained such material devastation. And anyway, there is no need for the identification of any crisis here, such that the divination of an apocalypse is necessary. No need for distasteful fear-mongering either. The clarity and confidence of our position already makes a claim to what follows—that no creation of a savior will be necessary. While the economic critique within the first half of this opuscule is built upon the ruins of industrialization, the proposal of the second is something of a compliment to a vision of the future—one that each and every one of us carries within us. We understand this vision as a proximal discourse which provides the conditions necessary for authenticity, such that truth may be encountered. The proposal will, however, be followed by a critical analysis of the prescriptions herein. This analysis will take the form of objections to the proposal. This is done in order to preemptively answer any immediate critics, particularly those who may notice that our proposal has been built upon an incomplete consideration of either theory or of factual historical evidence. Yet, despite our attempts to answer any potential critics by means of reasoning, we also understand that the proof of the correctness of our prescriptions falls outside the domain of facts and logic. The correctness of our prescriptions could only be proven in the soul, so to speak. Therefore, the objections are preceded by an exercise in three images. Now, it should be said, already here at the outset of this book, that in order to keep the manufacturing costs of this product down, and in an effort to produce a book which is both affordable and accessible, this exercise will require that you open the camera on your smart device; a QR code will take you to an artist's interpretation of our vision. While this type of exercise may at first appear unusual, dwelling within the artworks may produce the proof of our arguments, if you are predisposed with the ability to accept such aesthetic "proof" anyways. Together, the words and digital visualizations go hand-in-hand to embody a robust aesthetic—one which we can use as an idol as we press on ahead into our future.

Notes on Design and Appearance

Despite how it may seem at first, this opuscule is intended to be read by a general audience. Therefore, it should be understood that I have intended for there to be a certain obstruction in the design of this work—in the form of words from foreign languages. Be warned. Some words appearing throughout the historical economy of truth are not only foreign, but also from long deceased languages. This seemingly unnecessary difficulty affords me, as the author of this work, one security—that my reader may be unburdened by any modern prejudices which could undermine the intended experience of this work.

Of course, a translation of the Anglo-Saxon word *sōþ* (*sooth*), or Ancient Greek αληθεια into the Modern English *truth*, would expedite the processing of the text. However, this expediency carries with it the potential to cloud the exercise of interpretation. And, as in this case, the foreign word will do better. My reader should acknowledge, as I do, that the ancient texts which appear throughout the historical narrative are taken up for one purpose—clearing a space for philosophical reflection. Perhaps it is all-too easy to overlook the genuine philosophizing which occurs in translation of the exotic. Consider the exercise of importing even a living object such as the Korean *han* into the Anglo-American world. Inasmuch, it should be obvious that any dead object from ancient texts is material for rich reflection. Of course, I would be deceiving you if I promised to transport your way of thinking over to the ancients altogether. However, I have already resigned myself to the understanding that the economy in which those objects originated is long deceased. Therefore, I understand that the thought surrounding those objects is likewise impossible to reach. And, in any case, there is no benchmark which could decide, once and for all, a successful attempt here. Insofar as the value of this exercise falls outside the domain of falsifiability, I am not concerned if later evidence surfaces which disproves the content of the history.

On this account, I can prepare you for one task already now. You can expect that throughout the historical narrative of the economy of truth, you will be required to relearn words that may seem overly familiar to you. Therefore it must be said, despite my seeming disregard for your time and energy, I hope that you can enjoy, as I do, an estrangement from the overly familiar. Of course, it is undoubtable, today we favor works of art which are easily digestible. There is an expectation that all products conform to the standard demanded of the American commodities economy. However, if anyone does not find themselves in a position which favors the digestion of this work, then I maintain that it is not the work which is to be critiqued. Instead, I proceed with this work on the presumption that it is our condition which should fall to criticism. No doubt, an animation of "the global" exacerbates our anxieties for both ready-made answers and actions—certainly within the fields of political activism and economic reform. However, this anxiety is exactly what will come into question throughout this opuscule. Inasmuch, I can only hope that this work finds its way into the hands of those who can appreciate the reward which follows from difficulty. This work will undoubtedly resonate with those who understand that discovery is not only reserved to frontier exploration—and that elucidation is often more fertile ground than that of conquering the unknown.

However, this intended difficulty does raise one considerable alarm. I expect that the tempo of this work will depend entirely on the understanding which you, the reader, bring into this work. And so, unlike the nightclub DJ or stand-up comedian who can respond to his audience's mood with appropriate changes in tempo, I have had to forfeit such artistic control. I can only hope that digestion comes at an enjoyable pace. Note that for readers unfamiliar with either Ancient Greek or Latin, the last pages of this book present a glossary. Included within that glossary are the words which are taken up as specific terms within the architectonic of truth in the second half of this work.

One last note. I have been careful not to say too much about those fields of research where I am not an expert. While I fashion myself as something of a metaphysician (having found myself invested in the discipline for over ten years now), I am neither a translator of Ancient Greek nor Anglo-Saxon. In announcing this, I make no presumptions to the originality of this work's etymological datum. To this, I am in debt to the rich enlightenment from the researchers who have come before me. Before all else, this work should be read as a work of aesthetics. Its primary object is the metamodern aesthetic, which manifests through all activities of life and climaxes most jarringly within the political realm. Note that a bibliography follows the proposal. This serves to provide my reader with an understanding of the considerations which I have taken up in composing this opuscule.

—Justin Carmien, March 16th, 2020

The Historical Movement of Truth

Firstly, we ask ourselves, *what is truth*? This is a timeless philosophical question and, on that account, perhaps quite uninteresting as well "no"? The very appearance of the question provokes suspicion. We are weary to construe truth in such a fashion that our investigation becomes too narrow, thereby rendering our investigation easier, but less useful. We want "the whole truth and nothing but the truth!" as the expression goes. Yet at the same time, we should not be surprised that this is our initial question—after all, our investigation on *how to nurture truth and authenticity* demands that we delineate the object which guides our investigation. Of course, we can make a principal claim to this initial question. In asking after truth, we are not after *that which is true*—that is to say, any particular object of truth—but the very nature of truth itself. However, when thinking about this "nature", we need not heed to our concerns over the timelessness of this question. In asking about truth, we can proceed in much the same way we might seek to define *freedom* or *power*. Truth, just as with any other word, can be understood by looking at the economy to which it belongs—or more correctly, by looking at the recordings of testimony from within that economy. It is here that we find the meaning of words—this meaning pointing towards the nature of that object. Of course, in taking up this method for investigation, we should not worry about reducing truth to a mere dead word appearing in text. We do, after all, seek the identification of the very phenomena to which the word refers us. This method for defining terminological objects will be employed regularly throughout this opuscule. Therefore, perhaps some preliminary remarks on words, language, and objects are first in order.

It has been said that the world is constituted by the language which we take up in talking about it, and that this world is the total collection of objects talked about; and furthermore, that those objects themselves are nothing other than what we are able to say about them. Even when speaking of *the mysterious*, we say something about the constitution of that which is mysterious—we know it, as part of its very constitution, as a mystery. This is a constitutive understanding of language. Another argument suggests that language is much more biological—that it is *life* logical. Here, language is a tool. Much like the hammer that drives the nail, language disturbs the molecular composition of the air in order to affect another material object—a human ear, a human brain, a human body. However, we must also acknowledge that prior to such *language as material tool,* there also exists a ground for the possibility of language. That is, we must acknowledge the primordial condition from which language is possible. Following the work of German philosopher Martin Heidegger, we talk of this primordial condition as *discourse.*

Since discourse is a condition for language, it exists prior to language: it is pre-linguistic. As such, it is likely best expressed figuratively. Perhaps we could talk of discourse as something of a *harmony with nature* and only on account of this rhythmic harmony can the world come to be articulated as the world that it is. In this sense, we think of language (whether bodily, verbal, or written) as a mere refinement—a further-articulated form of discourse. For those who are more economically attuned, we might express this discourse as something of a pre-intellectual (or pre-cognitive, to use the scientific word) *wheeling and dealing with nature*; a *dealing* which takes place not only between people, but with the entirety of phenomena in experience.

This understanding puts this pre-intellectual *dealing* as that which is prior to material, or rather, as that which is a condition for material description. Now of course, no one would question that food is material—or that our whole biology could sustain itself without this sustenance. Yet, if we were not the type of thing that experienced hunger, then apples, blueberries or chunks of raw meat could never come to *be* food. It is not to say that other physical descriptions could not be obtained from those phenomena, but *food* could not be one of them. Likewise, a fallen tree could never come to *be* a chair if we were not the type of thing that enjoyed a relaxing pause after a hike through the woods. These very objects, be they *food* or *chair,* are conditioned by our very *wheeling and dealing* within our environment. Imagine, for example, an organism which, by way of its commerce within its environment, created definitions in that environment such that those definitions allowed for more articulated (and presumably more useful) commerce. Whether the organism of our consideration is some fantastical primordial ooze or simply a human baby, we can imagine the process of articulation—of drawing definition around sensual experiences—such that the organism could have in its possession *mom*, then *spoon*, and even the object *me*.

And yet, regarding this condition for language, another qualification must be made. This very handiwork activity of *wheeling and dealing with nature* is itself possible only on account of another condition—that which has been called *projection*. Perhaps we might think of projection by way of analogy to a physiological counterpart, like, for example, the previously mentioned hunger or perhaps even sexual drive, which "projects" towards sexual reproduction. However, we should not get caught up in analogies. Projection is that which conditions an orientation towards the future in its most robust sense. It conditions descriptions which provide for that future. For example, on an intellectual level, *the good* or *the just* are descriptions which provide for a realization of that goodness or that justice in the future. Projection, then, is the condition for the world to be encountered as the world which it is—whether the description which we come to is *wood, timber, toothpick, the good* or even *the truth*.

Looking into the rich history of human records we find testament to the many projects (projections) recorded by the human hand. Within that literature, we find not only a description of the material substrate with which they worked, but also the occult objects which facilitated an intellectual resolve to the hurdles which they faced. Throughout the *One-Thousand and One Arabian Nights*, for example, we find the disclosure of a causal-occult substrate—this substrate is with the purpose of reconciling with natural hierarchies. In those fairytales, we find appeals to *humility* before *Destiny* and praise to *God* for deliverance from the devastations of yet another deity, *Time, "the parter of companions and the destroyer of joy"*. Equally, we can find a similar substrate in the literature from the *medium aevum*—the European middle ages. Here we find literature by those who have fallen victim to the indifference of *Lady Fortune*, including the comfort of God's council—which has not only been taken up during creation, but has also been consulted when drawing up the blueprints of the end of times.

Despite all of this, it seems that *truth* feels like a meta-object. However, this feeling does not come to us on account of the utmost value which we place on it. Instead, truth feels like a meta-object because it stands as that which is to be disclosed as a whole, partly through each of those projects. Yet, despite this supposition, a light study of our historical texts reveals something quite contrary. What we know today by the name *truth* has been arrived at through a history of ascending and descending projects. Looking within the history recorded in English alone, we find texts which reveal that, long before truth was busy destroying the false, it was experienced as something of a light (it was a clarity of vision, so to speak)—one which was all-too susceptible to obscuration through the mists of doubt.

In the Anglo-Saxon world, we have an Old English text which reads,

> "Nu þu ne þeaɲɲc þe nauhc onðɲæðan. ɲoɲþam þe
> oɲ þam lȳclan ɲpeaɲcan ðe ðu mið þæɲe cȳnðɲan
> ᵹeɲenᵹe liɲeɲ leoht þe onliehce..."

> "oɲ þæm þonne onᵹinnað peaxan þa miɲcaɲ þe þ Moð
> ᵹeðɲeɲaþ. J mið ealle ɲoɲðpilmað þa ɲōþan ᵹeɲiehþe
> ɲpelce miɲcaɲ ɲpelce nu on ðinum Moðe ɲinðan..."

These words were transported into the Anglo-Saxon world by way of a translation of Roman senator Boethius' *De Consolatione Philosophiae* (*The Consolation of Philosophy*), circa 524 AD. Translated into Modern English by J.S. Cardale in 1829 we read,

"Now thou hast no need to fear any thing; for, from the little spark which thou hast caught with this fuel, the light of life will shine upon thee..."

"From hence, then, begin to grow the mists which trouble the mind, and entirely confound the true sight, such mists as are now on thy mind..."

The project which *The Consolation of Philosophy* is involved can be deciphered through the objects taken up in the language of the text. In the book, we read of *ſōþan ʒeſiehþe* ("the true sight"). Here, *ſōþan ʒeſiehþe* is what one has while dwelling in *ſōþ-an* ("the truth"). Only from this dwelling can the mists of doubt come to cloud over it. Of course, *ſōþ* is not to be understood as a spatial-temporal dwelling, but as a disposition from which the world is looked out to. This use of *ſōþ* is retained into Middle English, for example, in William Shakespeare's *Merchant of Venice*, "*In sooth, I know not why I am so sad*". That is to say, while dwelling in *ſōþ*, I have access to the knowledge of my sadness. Today, we find this idea of *truth as dwelling* quite alien. But only on account of these objects can we obtain the project of *The Consolation of Philosophy*. Disclosed through these objects, we find a quite peculiar encouragement of doubt. Doubt is promoted as a means to edification and, above all else, an assurance of God's counsel in the actualization of Fortune. Thus, we can interpret the project as one towards self-assurance. Of course, the need for self-assurance within this book is trivialized once we start to dwell on the Roman senator's life situation—after all, Boethius had been incarcerated for defending a treasonous senator. *The Consolation of Philosophy* is, therefore, undoubtedly a piece of prison literature. And of course, there is no better time for the self-assurance of consolation than during incarceration. Yet, despite this trivialization, what should not be underestimated is the book's popular appeal. *The Consolation of Philosophy* spread throughout the European continent. In this way, it can be said to resonate with the spirit of the *medium aevum*.

Of course, parallel to this understanding of truth as dwelling, we also interpret *rōþan ʒeſiehþe* as *the real sight*. In Modern English we retain this use, for example, in the expression *true love*. This expression also indicates something of a *false love*—a prior deception. Not to be overlooked, the true as *the real* also suggest *the one and only*. True love is undoubtedly single and sole—without comparison. This singularity retains in the conception of truth as an assertion which is in agreement with the real—*reality*. Inasmuch, we can say that it anticipates the foundation for the scientific industries. The French philosopher Rene Descartes, who has been called the father of the metaphysical foundations of modern science, began out of the same encouragement of doubt as a method for arriving at truth. However, in his work, assurance is explicitly absent. Instead, we find motivation for his method in certainty. The distinction between the two is essential in interpreting the novelty of Descartes's *Meditationes de Prima Philosophia* (*Meditations on First Philosophy*). While we could never understand what it would mean that nature would deceive us—with a fake atomic particle, say—we can follow the reasoning of Descartes in "subjectivizing" the deception. After all, we assume that nature has no preference whether or not we know it. Deception is a possibility of the thinker himself; therefore, the thinker's virtue is clarity of thought. Clarity is exclusive to reason. Inasmuch, we can say that certainty, in contrast to assurance, has the character of logical-mathematical. To be sure of this distinction, we can revisit Descartes's second meditation,

> "Our reason is not unjust when we conclude…that physics, astronomy, medicine and all other sciences…are very dubious and uncertain; but arithmetic, geometry and other science of that kind…contain some measure of certainty and an element of the indubitable. For whether I am awake or asleep, two and three together always form five, and the square can never have more than four sides, and it does not seem possible that truths so clear and apparent can be suspected of any falsity or uncertainty."

This passage is repeated here from a composite translation (from both French and Latin) by Elizabeth S. Haldane and G.R.T. Ross.

It is here, as the logical-mathematical, that we find a second and explicit utility which certainty secured. Undoubtedly, the projects of later modernization demanded unprecedented human mobilization. This mobilization was promised by an industrialization of human activity—an industrialization which could not have been possible without a logical-mathematical *standard*. During this period, the pervasiveness of standardization went unquestioned. This is attested for in the popularity of positivism as the guiding philosophy of the late-eighteenth and early-nineteenth centuries. Positivism takes the *positum*, the sensuous, as the real. Yet, positivism goes further than empiricism. The sensuous is that which constantly proves itself upon any appearance of doubt. Such proof can only be had by way of a subsequent verification—a repeatable verification. The *positum* is that which constantly proves itself by way of comparison with a *ruler of the standard*. The availability of the standard provides for the certainty whenever certainty is in question. The *positum* is verified data—"positive data"—the fact. In positivism, positive facts constitute the only genuine form of knowledge.

Of course, from the vantage point afforded to us today, what we find concerning are the verification of intimate objects such as those of subjective or aesthetic description. After all, it is not entirely clear what standard could be used for verification here. The Austrian philosopher Ludwig Wittgenstein interrogated this perplexity. Yet, his purpose was not merely to qualify the intimate objects of experience as different from those of scientific description—this much had been admitted for some time before him. Instead, Wittgenstein presents a series of arguments which suggest that this perplexity over standardization extends even to scientific investigation. In his own words, *"We learn to observe and to describe observations"*. That is, we are taught the scientific method. But he asks *"how is my own 'inner activity' checked in this case?"* That is, *"how will it be judged whether I really have paid attention* [to my sensations of the phenomena or not]*?"* (*Zettel*, section 426). To be clear, the purpose of his interrogation was not a destruction of scientific investigation outright, nor was it even an uprooting of the philosophical foundations for the sciences, but instead it was a philosophical elucidation. While measurement by way of a standard ruler is often given as reason for judgement, such reasoning must come to an end somewhere. Wittgenstein's elucidation becomes complete once we understand that even in standardization, a judgement must still be made. That is, we must still determine which standard to use,

> "If a blind man were to ask me 'Have you got two hands?' I should not make sure by looking. If I were to have any doubt of it, then I don't know why I should trust my eyes. For why shouldn't I test my eyes by looking to find out whether I see my two hands? What is to be tested by what?"

This passage from *On Certainty* (section 125) concludes with the question, *"Who decides what stands fast?"* In other words, who is to be the final judge? A God? A dictator? A technocrat? Society? Of course, with the failure of a grounding standard as the test for genuine knowledge, we must admit that at some point during the grounding of our reasons, we approach the very foundation of our reasoning—a *"rock bottom"*, as Wittgenstein called it. However, we should not misunderstand Wittgenstein's elucidation as a criticism, such that we are reduced to either the irrational or occult. Instead, what we find at such a rock bottom is not faith (Wittgenstein is not promoting Christianity, for example) but conviction—or rather the economy in which we find our convictions. This is what Wittgenstein means when he says that *"It is what human beings say that is true and false; and they agree in the language they use. That is not agreement in opinions but in form of life"*. (*Philosophical Investigations,* Part I, section 241). Only a *form of life* could determine the final judge—an ultimate ruler of the standard. Of course, when thinking about the form of life, we are nearly brought full circle again, and back to the very inception of this chapter and our reflections on our primordial discourse and projection.

Despite this elucidation, we do recognize within ourselves a want for truth as the positive fact. Therefore, we also understand this conception as our own today. However, we can also say that Wittgenstein has prepared us for our task. Much like the mark of a snow angel which is left by waving one's arms and legs, we search for the economy—that form of life—which is impressed upon each and every one of us in having the truth of matters decided by way of the positive fact. Let us refrain from burdening ourselves with presumptions at this point. Evidence for this form of life is nothing yet, besides the positive fact itself. Yet, we should also remind ourselves of the original provocations that led up to this investigation—a feeling that in some way we have not done a satisfactory job of nurturing the disclosure of truth from within our inherited economy. We go forward with the understanding that any deception, dissimulation, or concealment of truth has only surfaced as a by-product of our interpersonal commerce. We likewise understand that nothing interesting can come from looking at dissimulation, deception, and concealment as deviations from normal behavior from within our inherited infrastructure.

From the vantage point of the liminal *here* and *now* of our present moment, it has become blatantly apparent that maintaining the positive fact has perversely obscured authenticity. When looking back to recent modernization, we find the intimate objects of subjective or aesthetic description bullied out of conversation—relegated to secondary objects, if respected at all. Evidently, internet forums became platforms for pedantic concerns over the qualification of the nature of truth. For those who cared to look closely enough, we found the project to discern *opinion* from *fact* and *believing* from *knowing*—that is to say, to discern between belief, fact, and *believing in facts*. This was an attempt at the reconciliation of the language inherited through the poets and ancient philosophers. While *the true* was equivalent to fact and opposite to *opinion* and *belief*—all that we really wanted to say was that the true is tantamount to that which is verified with a third-party "objective" reality. This is an understanding of the faculty of truth taking for granted the *thing-in-itself*, Immanuel Kant's metaphysical object, *noumenon*.

Yet today, this resolution has proven itself to be unsatisfactory. Undoubtedly, the proclamation "Truth!" discloses more than simply verifiable phenomena. Behind this statement is the value "good!" or "healthy!"—it is a testament to "an affirmation of my life!" Even the positive fact carries value—a utility which was utterly obscured in, for example, the United States abortion debate. It seems the positive fact had become a shield—one which protected the speaker and concealed *the good* and *the just*. We simply resolved that, "I can't dispute the facts", and we did this with our shoulders shrugged. We wrote away the profundity of our experiences—and with them the project (projection) to which our descriptions referred. As we go forward in searching for our form of life, we must say, already now, we should not expect that our prescriptions for nurturing authenticity will be directed towards nurturing the disclosure of the fact. And after all, we must admit that prescriptions here would be quite uninteresting. This opuscule would have never been written if it were done so with the intention of simply prescribing the establishment of better institutions for empirical investigation. For the time being, we can assume that our economy itself can no longer satisfy our content. We conclude this chapter only as an initiation for what follows.

Αλήθεια, Verum, Truth

Our project, as per the title of this opuscule, is to nurture truth and authenticity. In order to do so, we must discover the economy in which truth is in service of today. Only with such an identification can we understand our original provocation—an unsatisfactory commitment to the disclosure of truth. And only then will we be prepared for making a reform proposal. While we have identified truth as the positive fact, we have yet to identify the *essence* of the economy to which the positive fact belongs. Of course, in asking for *the essential economy*, we are not looking for an answer such as *capitalism* or *market economics*. We should remain confident that answers such as these would prove to be unsatisfactory. We are here doing *first economics*. As such, we seek identification of a common characteristic in both capitalism and market economics, or any other *dealing* which makes use of the positive fact. This essence cannot be reducible to either physiological or psychological motivations such as profit, prestige, or political influence. Though, the essence could be used to explain such motivations. And, to be sure, the essence which we seek is obscured by such explanations. Therefore, in order to identify what is essential in the economy of the positive fact, we must reach further back into history. While this may seem like a roundabout way to arrive at economic reform prescriptions today, we should remain confident and steadfast in our methodology. It is self-evident that capitalism and market economics did not spring into existence themselves. By transporting ourselves through history, we will find ourselves more and more estranged from these labels, to the point where we can be delivered over to an understanding of their essence.

We begin by following the etymology of *rōþ*, a process which we began in the previous chapter. While *rōþ* has fallen out of parlance, another word (one with a different etymological heritage) *triewþ* ("truth") remains in use all the way up to and including the Modern English we now use. But this was not before *rōþ* had found a home in another *dealing*—one which remains preserved in the word *soothsayer*. A soothsayer is one who speaks fantastically and without justification, insofar as divination is an ill-respected profession today. Therefore, we can say that *rōþ* did not become obsolete; rather, it has switched meanings. So for the time being, let us forget *rōþ* and direct ourselves to the Middle English origins of our object truth. Here we find very similar words such as *trouthe, truthe, trewthe*, and *treowthe*. Furthermore, this family of words can be traced back to the Anglo-Saxon words *trēowþ* and *trīewþ*. Despite the appearance of obsolete characters in these words, the Modern English *truth* is still recognizable. And while there is not a single definition to contain the meaning, we can say that the context of the Anglo-Saxon's texts directs us towards associations with Modern English words such as *veracity, faith, fidelity, loyalty, honor, pledge,* and *covenant*. We can follow this etymology further back to the Proto-Germanic *triwwiþō* ("promise, covenant, contract"). From here, we find the Proto-Indo-European **drū-* ("tree") and **deru-*

("firm, solid"). Additionally, we find modern *truth* cognate with Norwegian *trygd* ("trustworthiness, security, insurance"), Icelandic *tryggð* ("loyalty, fidelity"). All of this can be researched on Wiktionary.com in greater detail than is worth printing in this book. However, a particular absence becomes strikingly apparent with only this shallow etymological interrogation—an absence which tells us that this might be the wrong place for investigation into the essential economy in which truth is employed today.

What is spoken today in the word "truth!" is only in a very narrow sense *fidelity, loyalty,* or *promise.* Today, what we mean by the word truth, as the positive fact, undoubtedly refers to something much more concrete. It is *the real, the one and only.* This is the sense in which truth can refer us to the material substrate of physics. What should not be overlooked is that this essence of truth has meaning in relation to the false—and in looking at the Anglo-Germanic etymology of *truth,* this relationship is explicitly absent. Inasmuch, we can conclude that the essence of our Modern English word *truth* is of very un-Germanic origins. Instead, this dichotomic paradigm of the true/false can be traced to the social and political revolution preceding the *medium aevum*—the Christianization of Europe. Of course, we might ask ourselves, *could Christianization have had enough force to transform the very conception of truth among a people?* Undoubtedly, we should answer "yes". And, after all, we should expect nothing less from a transformation of pagan culture. In order to understand this transformation, we must look towards the authority of the Holy Roman Empire and the language of the Church. In Latin, we discover the dichotomic essence—*verum* ("true") and *falsum* ("false"). Interrogating this origin of truth further is paramount for understanding the service which truth, as the positive fact, came to fulfill.

We translate the Latin *verum* into Modern English as *the true*. The stem of *verum* is *ver*. In tracing the history of *ver*, etymologists have identified the Indo-European root *per*. Even in mouthing these two sounds we notice a correspondence. Now, understanding *per* in English is actually quite easy. These three letters most likely come forward to an English speaker as a prefix. Looking at words such as *pervert, pervade,* and *perfect,* the prefix directs us to associations with *through, thoroughly,* or *throughout.* However, we also find *per* leading the word *percent.* Here, *per* not only parses a whole, but also serves to establish something of a spatial or temporal boundary. Only by means of both *through* and *boundary* can the essential economy preserved within this root come forward. In English, *per* is preserved in the word *experience.* We can think of experience as that which is the boundary of a person's day-to-day life, their village, their tribe, and so on. However, experience not only parses a boundary in order to simply have that designation. *My* experience and *your* experience present themselves when that boundary is at issue—only when I am present with experience as an obstacle, one which must be transcended. The word *experience* owes itself to an encounter with a boundary such that there can be movement not only throughout, but also through and beyond it. Therefore, we can come to think of *per* as belonging to the economy of *parsing to transcend.* Perhaps we might say, *to divide and conquer.*

With the essential economy of *per* explicated, the domain to which the Roman Christian *verum* belongs also presents itself. The proclamation "*verum!*" draws definition in the phenomenal experience. The phenomena bound by that definition we know as true, but this designation does not come forward for the sake of merely obtaining in knowledge. The utility of *verum* presents itself only when looking to transcend the definition. Quite figuratively, we might say that *verum* is a building block. The thorough, throughout, and throughness of *verum* reveals a project concerned with the construction of an *empire of knowledge*. Therefore, in *verum*, we read an implicit comportment towards phenomena in general—an approach towards phenomena for the sake of appropriation into the dominion of knowledge.

Now, we can bring ourselves into a moment of profound elucidation if we follow the utility of *verum* through the economy of the empire. Yet, this moment can only be fully realized if we understand the dichotomy in which *verum* belongs. After all, only in understanding the two components can the whole be brought into meaning. In *falsum* we find *fallo*. Etymologists have traced Latin *fallo* to the reconstructed language of Proto-Indo-European. Here we find **(s)gʷʰh₂el-*, meaning *to stumble*. The second-person singular future-passive indicative of *fallo* is *fallere—to bring to a fall*. However, where is this *falsum*, this *bringing to a fall*, essential within the economy of the empire? What realm of experience is normative here? This question is not particularly novel, although it seems to have failed to produce much excitement within academia. Inasmuch, it has remained obscure to a popular, mainstream audience. Despite this, it is high time that we repeat this question. After all, we are operating today from within larger empires than any other which we might find in our history books and other such sources. Understanding the essential economy of *verum* and *falsum*—the essential economy of the true and the false—is of paramount importance for diagnosing the symptoms of modernization. Therefore, in going back to the origin, we find the question delivered over to us by way of its pronouncement by Martin Heidegger. Of course, the question already contains an answer in itself, and Heidegger himself answers his own question by reference to the colonial history of the post-Iron Age Mediterranean. His narrative follows,

> "Command as the essential ground of domination, includes being-superior, which is only possible as the constant surmounting of others, who are thereby the inferiors. In this surmounting there resides again the constant ability to oversee. We say where to 'oversee' something means to 'dominate' it. This overseeing includes the surmounting, involves a constant 'being-on-the-watch'. That is the form of acting which oversees everything but still keeps to itself: in Latin the *actio* of the *actus*…The essence of the *imperium* resides in the *actus* of constant 'action'. The imperial action of the constant surmounting of others includes the sense that the others, should they rise to the same or even to a neighboring level of command will be brought down—in Latin *fallere* (participle: *falsum*)…The properly great feature of the imperial resides not in war but in the *fallere* of subterfuge as round-about action and in the pressing-into-service for domination…the *falsum* is treachery and deception, 'the false.'"

Heidegger's narrative comes to us by way of Richard Rojcewicz and André Schuwer's translation of *Gesamtausgabe*, volume 54. This volume is comprised of material taken from a series of hour-long lectures which Heidegger conducted during the winter term of 1942-1943 at the University of Freiburg. While the narrative goes unexemplified in the lecture course material, the interpretation of *falsum* still resonates today. We can find supporting narratives running through Theodor Mommsen's multiple book-length magnum opus, *History of Rome*. According to the Greek way of thinking, it was a polite method of acquiring influence over powerful barbarians who would not submit to *imperium* ("command"), to treat them as if they were of Greek extraction. This was not only an admirable refinement to flattery, but also a deceptive kind of political trickery. The myths of Roman settlements trace their heritage to a Trojan colony. Therefore, for the Romans themselves, subterfuge would have been a social substrate which laid the foundations of their very city. Following Julius and Augustus Caesar, *ius Latii* ("Roman Rights") were used in a similar way—as a political instrument that aimed at the integration of provincial communities. We should not be surprised, then, if the *falsum* took its essence from the realm of Roman *imperium* in the form of the *fallere*—the false, that which is a deception—of subterfuge.

Now, we may be tempted to judge this etymology as merely material suitable for trivial pursuits—a narrative only useful for entertaining afternoon coffee partners; hardly material for making economic reform prescriptions. And at this juncture, we might find ourselves inquiring into not only Heidegger's ambition, but also the relevance of his project to the one which we are undertaking here. After all, what kind of imperialism bothers us here? Are we not talking about knowledge? And isn't the project of a certain *epistemic imperialism* healthy? More confusedly we might ask, *what other projects could we expect truth to serve?* And make no mistake, these are all good questions. They will inform the investigation through the next few pages, as well as the next three chapters, concluding the first half of this opuscule.

Heidegger's lecture course in question was called *Parmenides* and *Heraclitus*, but in light of the nearly exclusive occupation with Parmenides' didactic poem on the goddess Αληθεια, the editors modified the title of the volume to

Parmenides in publication. From the very first pages of this volume, we find Heidegger eager to transport his students' thinking from any modern prejudices. His ambition is to wrench Ancient Greek αλήθεια of any associations which our translation into *truth* provokes. This is in order to redeem Parmenides' goddess from the Latinization which dominates our interpretation today.

The next three passages from the lecture course material will give us three words to work with in understanding Heidegger's project: **αληθευειν** (*alētheuein* "to adhere to the unconcealed disclosive in the saying that lets appear"), **ομοιωσις** (*homoiosis*, "the disclosive correspondence expressing the unconcealed"), and **οιεσθαι** (*iesthē*, "to take something as something"),

> "Since Plato, and above all by means of Aristotle's thinking, a transformation was accomplished within the Greek essence of αλήθεια, one which in a certain respect αλήθεια itself encouraged."
>
> "Αλήθεια is the unconcealed and disclosing."
>
> "The unconcealed can be disclosed by humans and for humans only if their comportment adheres to the unconcealed and is in agreement with it. Aristotle uses the word αληθευειν for this comportment… This adherence to and agreement with the unconcealed is in Greek ομοιωσις. This correspondence takes and holds the unconcealed for what it is. To take something for something is in Greek οιεσθαι…"

While it has become trivial to acknowledge that "the subjective" was a concept foreign to the Ancient Greeks, it nonetheless requires a special attunement to experience ourselves out of this very modern conception. In the above three passages, we find Heidegger's ομοιωσις ("the disclosive correspondence expressing the unconcealed") as an "event" which occurs outside the subjective realm. It may be helpful to imagine this event by way of the so-called "theory of forms" and Plato's ειδος or ιδεα (*idea*). Taking an example of a chair, we could say that ομοιωσις ("making like") presences the ιδεα "chair" as the particular chair that it is. Ομοιωσις is ecstatic. Either the phenomena presents itself as what it is, or it presents itself in the form of a guise, or ψευδης (*pseudōs*). Nature is here understood as *that which shows itself, as it is, of itself.* There is no "human subject" mediating ομοιωσις. Now, while this return to the ancients and along with it a collapse of the subject/object dichotomy may seem backwards to scientific ways of thinking, Heidegger is interested in qualifying scientific investigation as one *type of human project*, one which has obscured the more robust "human" experiences of the ancients. Therefore, Heidegger is concerned with the Latinization of Greek culture and language. And more importantly, the obscuration of Parmenides' Αληθεια by way of a Latinization which then set the course for history—a course which has displaced truth from its home in the "objective" domain (or, in remaining consistent with a pre-modern way of thinking, simply what we call *nature*),

> "*Imperium* is commandment, command. The Roman Law—*ius*—*iubeo*—is rooted in the same essential domain of the imperial, command, and obedience. Command is the ground of the essence of domination...But now because *verum* is counter to *falsum*, and because the essential domain of the *imperium* is decisive for *verum* and *falsum* and their opposites, the sense of *ver*, becomes maintaining...*verum* be-

49

> comes forthwith 'being-above', directive of what is
> right; *veritas* is then *rectitudo*, 'correctness'."

> "But because the Greek *ομοιωσις* turned into *rectitu-*
> *do*, the realm of *αληθεια*, disclosure, still present for
> Plato and Aristotle in *ομοιωσις*, disappeared."

The Latin *rectitudo* ("rightness, correctness") was understood by Heidegger as *"the self-adjusting to"*. Today, after
many centuries of refinement, we have the object the *hu-*
man subject to contain this event. This self-adjusting, or
correction, or, perhaps more interestingly, *being correct* is
explicitly apparent in the scientific method, for example. Of
course, what should be noted is that Heidegger is not criti-
cizing the sciences outright. However, *αληθεια*, as pure and
primordial *unconcealment*, as that which is immediately
present (specifically as *the beautiful, the good,* and *the just*)
is uprooted. What we would know today as *the truth*, as an
aesthetic description towards *the good*, is wrenched from its
original domain in nature. And what we find preserved in
the historical record of the Latinization of Ancient Greek
culture, presented to us here by way of Heidegger's lecture
course material, is a preparation such that truth could be
studied by means of anthropology and sociology—that is,
relative from the position of the omniscient world observer.
There can be no doubt, then, that the ground had been laid
for nihilism, announced by Friedrich Nietzsche many centuries following.

Returning now to our historical economy of truth; although
we began with the Holy Roman Empire and the Christian
transformation of the Anglo-Germanic conception of truth,
it is now only a matter of enumeration to complete the
history of truth and its use within the economy of *imperi-*
um's domination. We can trace the dichotomic essence of

truth as the positive fact from the various scientific industries back to Rene Descartes, the father of the metaphysical foundations of modern science. Undoubtedly, Descartes's metaphysics not only laid the foundations for modern science, but it also transported *verum's* utility within imperial economy. *Imperium,* the command, was transported from the Pope, who commanded the truth through, for example, the Spanish Inquisition, over to the authorities within the scientific industries. Since we have already admitted that language articulates the world, we should not be surprised to find the language of Latin—constructed during the establishment and maintenance of imperial economy—as that which contains within it the essential economy of modernization. Truth exists, even today, as the positive fact, as that which *parses to transcend,* within the same essential economy. This economy seeks to build an empire by way of *the one and only* domain of the true and the false. And although we might be proud to have wrested the *I command the truth* from the hands of the priests of Catholicism, we should not be surprised over the abuse of truth in later times—in the form of fake news or alternative facts. Our infrastructure is built to maintain this essential economy. Truth is in service to command. Therefore, there can be no doubt that, as a consequence, we have developed a perverse relationship towards the disclosure of truth, generally.

Of course, we also have the right to be suspicious of *this* particular conclusion. After all, no matter how elucidating this historical narrative may be, can we really remain satisfied with this identification alone? Truth in the hands of commandment?—so what? Do we not simply have recourse, once again, to psychology? It is tempting, here and now, to diagnose our *"perverse relationship towards disclosure"* by means of the psychological toolkit. According to this logic, the pursuit of the human animal's physiological needs, now satiated, manifests as psychosis—*greed* and *selfishness*. In this case, it is not commandment itself, but *commanding for too much* which is to blame. This psychosis then accounts for our dissatisfaction with deception, dissimulation, and the concealment of the truth in our contemporary economy. However, we should remind ourselves that the psychological diagnoses exist for *correcting* degeneration from normal behavior. And what should not be overlooked is that *greed* and *selfishness* are not only appropriate descriptions to phenomena, but that those descriptions themselves belong to our economy, our *form of life* today. Of course, this is not to say that psychological descriptions such as *greed* or *selfishness* could not accurately describe phenomena in every human economy of the past, present, or future. But taking up a higher vantage point, we allow ourselves some perspective. Consider that today we *could* call to archaic causal-occult objects such as *luck* for explaining our phenomenal experience—but, in all honesty, do we really think that it is helpful to do so? And yet, that description was helpful at some time, in some economy. Objects such as *luck, greed,* and *selfishness* are living. As such, they have the possibility of becoming extinct. We should be careful of policing deviant cases by way of psychology and on account of an apparent absolutism of descriptions such as *greed* and *selfishness*. This can only derail us from more fruitful tasks. Instead, we are searching for the condition which gives rise to the products of our economy—both to those which we cherish and those which we abhor. We understand that they belong to a complete package.

Epistemology, the Metaphysics of Colonialism

Epistemology—from Ancient Greek επιστημη (*epistēmē*, "science, knowledge") and λογια (*logia*, "discourse").

Epistemology—the discourse of knowledge.

Where do our thoughts take us when we are presented with only this provisional translation of epistemology?

When thinking of an answer to the above query, we may want to look closer at "episteme-", and thereby assume the "-ology" as a given. After all, the suffix "-ology" is overly familiar to all of us, of course. We have *sociology, psychology, anthropology,* and the many other disciplines and subdisciplines both familiar and obscure, which all focus on their respective subject matter. However, we should not be too dismissive. There are depths worth exploring in both halves of this word. It is within those depths, and by way of a further interrogation into epistemology, that we will progress our historical narrative of the economy of truth as initiated in the previous chapters. This interrogation will provide us with the necessary language required for thematizing a primordial "action" and comportment towards the world—

that which we will name *episteme*. While episteme is a word which traces back to the Ancient Greeks, we will give it a novel qualification in this chapter. And while this undertaking may firstly strike the reader as quite audacious, our qualification will allow for an understanding of the reification of the metaphysical "subject" and of the causal-occult object *power* within the Western tradition—an understanding which we will use to identify "subjectivity" and diagnose the cause of *"our perverse relationship to disclosure"* as announced in the previous chapter. Therefore, let us now continue our interrogation into epistemology by way of an etymological study, beginning where we left off, with the suffix, "-ology".

As has already been suggested, this suffix comes to us through the Ancient Greek λογια. However, λογια also refers to λογος (*logos*). Now, the utility which λογος has served its authors is admittedly so diverse that we cannot contain its meaning in a single Modern English word. On Wikitionary.com, we find λογος referred to as *speech, oration, discourse, quote, story, study, ratio, word, calculation,* and *reason.* Therefore, we must conclude that λογος can only be understood from within the text in which we find it. From the fragments which have been ascribed to Heraclitus, for example, λογος seems to have referred to an object. *"All things come to be in accordance with logos."* In this sense, "-ology" does not refer us to λογια (as a disciplinary subject), but to that by which phenomena come into accord with one another. We find a related type of reification of λογια in modern parlance. Biology, for example, not only refers to βιο-λογια (as the disciplinary subject), but also to that by which phenomena come into accord with one another—namely, βιο-λογος. Only in conforming to βιο-λογος could the phenomena of an organism's biology present itself as that biology. This understanding of "-ology" as both λογια ("discourse") and λογος ("that by which phenomena come into accord with one another") will soon prove useful as we proceed into our qualification of epistemology.

Continuing with our etymological interrogation, let us now turn our attention to the root "episteme-"; again, we find επιστημη. This word is itself from the Ancient Greek επισταμαι (epistamai)—a compound of επι (epi, "upon, over, above") and ιστημι (histēmi, "to make stand"). Therefore, in taking up this etymological foundation, we translate επιστημη, quite literally, as *to make over-stand*.

Now, while this "translation" of episteme is etymologically sound, we should also admit that it does not follow from the meaning which we read from the Ancient Greek writers. Within the works of Plato, Aristotle, and others, episteme is more appropriately translated into either *science* or *knowledge* in Modern English, as had already been suggested at the beginning of this chapter. Therefore we ask ourselves, *what can a translation of episteme as "to make overstand" do for us now, specifically in furthering our understanding of epistemology,* since even for the Ancient Greeks this sense was not apparent? With regards to this question, we must keep in mind that the discipline of epistemology is, for us today, a specific discipline which arose following Descartes's *prima philosophia* of the seventeenth century; it was first articulated as such by the German philosopher Christian Wolff in the eighteenth century. Therefore, in seeking to qualify epistemology, we must admit that we are seeking to qualify something which is, after all, quite foreign and removed from the Ancient Greeks and their way of thinking. And, for us, this discrepancy in thinking between the Ancients and the epistemologists of the seventeenth century is quite significant.

In the lecture course material which we drew from in the last chapter, namely *Parmenides and Heraclitus*, we find Martin Heidegger preparing his students for understanding a transposition of λογος (following Heraclitus, as *that to which phenomena accord*) into human reason by way of a Latinization of Ancient Greek language and culture. From the vantage point afforded to us today, and while following the directive of Heidegger's lecture course material, we cannot help but describe what seems to be an overly-obvious history. This Latinization of the language of the Ancient Greeks is the historical pivot which prepares us for bridging episteme (*as to make overstand*) to epistemology,

> "To take something for something is in Greek οιεσθαι..."
>
> "The λογος is constituted by οιεσθαι..."

However,

> "To take something as something is in Latin *reor*—the corresponding noun is *ratio*...[However, with the advent of a Latinization of Greek culture] the essence of truth as *veritas* and *rectitudo* passes over in the *ratio* of man...This determines for the future, as a consequence of a new transformation of the essence of truth, the technological character of modern, i.e., machine, technology. And that has its origin in the originating realm out of which the imperial emerges. The imperial springs forth from the essence of truth as correctness in the sense of the directive self-adjusting guarantee of the security of domination. The taking as true of *ratio*, of *reor*, becomes a far-reaching and

anticipatory security. *Ratio* becomes counting, calculating, calculus."

What is significant for us then, particularly in recounting
our historical economy of truth by way of an interrogation
of epistemology, is exactly this *"self-adjusting guarantee of
the security of domination"*. With the inception of the epistemological project in the seventeenth century, we find a description of experience such that phenomena are brought
into accord through a self-adjusting "subject" indicated by
the "I, myself". This subject "apprehends" phenomena—but
this apprehension is not merely the act of sensual perception. Apprehension suggests a stronger sense—as in, for
example, when we say, "the suspect has been apprehended
by the police". Phenomena are apprehended into custody,
and in such apprehension the *I* is likewise asserted. Looking
back into history, Descartes's writing might be considered
as an inception of the "subjectivist" historical paradigm—a
paradigm which we will now take up, as we follow our own
historical narrative, under construction now. However, before proceeding, we should also be clear. This "apprehension into custody" was also known by the Ancient Greeks.
In their writing we find κτῆσις (*ktēsis*, "appropriation, possession"). Therefore, it must be said that what is novel within the description offered to us by the epistemologists is the
unquestionable substantiality of doubt, overstanding, and
will, together as represented by the self-adjusting subject, *I*.

Recalling Descartes's second meditation, we read,

> "It is so self-evident that it is I who doubts, who *over-
> stands*, and who desires, that there is no reason here
> to add anything to explain it."

We therefore conclude. The subject, *I*, to which *doubt, over-standing*, and *desire* is invested, is at once both the condition and the conclusion. Doubt conditions επιστημη, but it also presupposes the outcome, επιστημη, on the basis of a deficiency of επιστημη. In each of these uses, both *knowledge* and *to make overstand* are interchangeable. Doubt is not only the condition for knowledge, it is also the foundation for "being one's self". And this description of one's self as "the subject" has the character of a machine-like self-propelled engine.

In tracing this "*far-reaching and anticipatory security of domination*", we come to Immanuel Kant, nearly one-hundred and fifty years following Descartes. Within Kant's voluminous philosophical works, we again find the subject, *I*, as the indubitable location of *doubt, overstanding*, and *desire*. However, we also find a more articulate and refined science. To Descartes's trinity of doubt, overstanding, and desire, we can then add, before all else, the *noumenon* ("thing-in-itself"). Within Kant's *Critique of Pure Reason*, we are told the story of how a subject (that same subject of Descartes's *prima philosophia*) "transcends" its subjectivity in order to apprehend the *noumenon*. Of course, with the logical-mathematical character of the world being married, so to speak, to empirical practice, this then makes possible a description of objects with definite edges—ones which butt right up next to one another, such that every mental and physical space could be accounted for. Following Kant's reconciliation of rationalism with empiricism, the world was prepared for a certain *epistemic imperialism*—a mastering, a conquering and, above all, a "totaling" of an objectified "uni-verse"—that single and sole quantifiable reality.

Now, we understand quite simply that knowledge does not include in itself any particular *red apple*, say, but instead the descriptions *red* and *apple*. Physics, for example, does not include in itself *gravity*, but is instead the discipline which contains both the atemporal and aspatial description *gravity*. Therefore, we can say that the objects of knowledge, of episteme, are both atemporal and aspatial—that is to say, they are *universal* in character. If we then take episteme as both a primordial "action" and also as the character of the apprehending of the phenomenal experience, then the universality of episteme reveals itself to be totalitarian in character. And while the work of both Descartes and Kant are genuine in their pursuits to describe the primordial conditions of intellectual apprehension (a description which apparently goes back to the Ancient Greeks and, in particular, to Plato, and to his articulations on κτησις as they appear in, for example, the *Sophist*), we can also understand the works of these early epistemologists as a testament to the very human project of domination—a project which also manifested contemporarily as colonialism, following the age of exploration. Of course, we may be hesitant, and perhaps think it a bit strange, to proclaim the metaphysicians of the middle and late second millennium as having expedited imperial activity. However, we need not worry ourselves too much. We are also satisfied if, today, we find their work as a *mere* indication and testament to a current running through later modernization—one which provokes our thoughts further towards a historical narrative. This claim will become further supported in subsequent chapters as we trace episteme, thusly defined, through our political history up to our present time. However, what is required, before proceeding any further into that history, is a bit of terminological clarity—specifically, we must define, for ourselves, the discipline to which our new terminology, *episteme*, belongs.

It must be said that when we speak of a "*primordial comport-ment*", we are not speaking of an action within the realm of physics and mechanical cause-and-effect. Instead, this word "primordial" refers to the condition of possibility, including the possibility of causality. To make this clear, we only need to consider that the "apprehension" of episteme allows for an "objectification" of phenomena, such that we can speak of the objects of the world intellectually—whether those objects are of a material category, including *food* and *chairs*, or whether they are of a moral category, including *feminism* and *liberty*. This primordial comportment is, therefore, prior to any *being there* of the world; or, as it is also known, and in the terminology of Kant, *a priori*. That is to say, as an explanation of the conditions for the world *to be known*, episteme belongs to a description which is prior to even physics. As such, this comportment belongs to a *pre-physical* description. Episteme is an object which belongs to *metaphysical description*. Because this distinction between the physical and the metaphysical will soon become important in our development, let us call metaphysical "action" by the Latin word which we took up in the previous chapter, *actio* ("act of doing or making"), for terminological clarity.

Having now identified the primordial *actio* of *to make over-stand*, that which is manifest in the episteme of epistemolo-gy, we can recount the history of the economy of truth from the last chapter. By way of appropriation into an economy whose essence is that of *parse to transcend*, Ancient Greek ομοιωσις was Latinized into *rectitudo*. Λογος then passed over into the *ratio* of man. By way of Latinization, λογος becomes reason. And the idolization of reason expedit-ed a counting, calculating, and calculus throughout later modernization. This narrative can be traced throughout the Roman Empire, Christendom, and the epistemological project of Descartes and Kant, among others. The language of Latin, which carries within it the monological essence of the imperial, had become the foundation of the international industrialized sciences—which took hold of the true and false for understanding *the real* and *the one and only*. And while the epistemological project seems to have ended in earnest at the beginning of the twentieth century with Edmund Husserl, the climax of the imperial narrative is to be found a few decades later. We only need to revisit the construction of the world's superpowers in the twentieth century, the space race, and the pride which the victors felt in the accomplishment of NASA's Apollo 11 mission. After all, this project produced one of the most striking images of modernization, the United States flag standing on the moon. There is likely no better image which indicates the transcendent *actio* of episteme. And yet, there is an opportunity for us *here* and *now*, equipped with this imperial narrative, to interpret this image in an even more fulfilling way.

While the precedent of naming manned spaceflight projects after mythological gods had already been set with Mercury, Abe Silverstein, Director of Space Flight Development, found the imagery of Apollo, the sun god traveling across the cosmos in his chariot, to be an appropriate association. However, what is uncanny is that for the Romans, Apollo was not only the sun god, he was also the god who presided over the colonists. The colonies of Antiquity were post-Iron Age city-states founded from a mother city. While Greek colonies were often founded to solve social unrest in the mother city by expelling a part of the population, Roman colonies were used for expansion and empire building. Apollo was the giver of laws, and his oracles were consulted before setting laws in the city. And so, even if the name *Apollo* was chosen quite arbitrarily for the spaceflight project, the temptation is still irresistible. Today, we find *imperium* invested into this name. Apollo, our god of colonists, is at the same time our god of episteme—which has not only guided our vision as we pushed the boundary of the frontier and expanded the empire, but did so in the name of apprehension and overstanding knowledge. Today, in this *"time between worlds"*, we read the image of the United States flag on the moon as a slightly appalling perversion of the humble condition of doubt.

Now, of course, having brought one the most celebrated icons of modernization into ill-association, we also deserve a bit of hesitation towards this imperial narrative and its conclusions. Perhaps we feel a bit of dissonance. After all, some apprehension is good "no"? And we might want to believe, as we always have, that what should be in question is not apprehension, but right judgement. Besides, we are forfeit to our own nature "no"? And episteme directs our orientation towards the world in general. Only on account of our apprehension of phenomena can the world be, whatsoever. So, we have no other alternative; we must strive for right judgement. Feed the poor. Save the environment. Lock up the bad guys. This is the story which we are wont to reason.

At this juncture, we should not resent such dissonance. After all, it is only a sign of a lack of clarity; we have not yet considered our historical narrative thoroughly enough. And of course, our historical narrative of the economy of truth is pronouncedly incomplete. We are nowhere near the *here* and *now* of today. There are undoubtedly a few hundred years left to account for before we arrive at episteme as it presents itself today, most explicitly, through our spirit for *liberalism*. However, without getting too ahead of ourselves, as tempting as that may be, we must follow the program of our development and first consider those *"few hundred years"*. Now, if we are to remain true to our method, then we must take the testimony of our historical continuum as our directive. Although we must admit that it is superficial to lump many diverse projects together, thus destroying what is essential to each one, it is nevertheless a survey which we are interested in at this moment. Therefore, in referencing the texts following the European epistemologists, we find ourselves confronted with a pervasive anthropomorphism—that is, a humanization of the world founded upon the epistemologist's *I*. While we might dissect the various philosophies of thinkers such as G.W.F. Hegel or Friedrich Nietzsche, it is perhaps Arthur Schopenhauer's philosophy which is an obvious case of such anthropomorphism. In his philosophy the world is explicitly expressed as *will*. And if we understand these texts as constituting Western philosophy proper, then it seems that the entirety of Western thinking had taken up the reified metaphysical object *power*. Of course, even if this is the case, some very clever people may be quick to remind us that the world is always "anthropological", in that it is always spoken of through the human mouth. And, in such a case, the world itself is always an "anthropomorphism". Of course, we cannot argue against this reasoning. However, there is one understanding which we would do well to remind ourselves of. The object *power*, as treated of within the discipline of physics, is different from the power which is treated of within mathematics—and both of these objects are different from the causal-occult *power* which is treated of within the discipline of sociology. Therefore, the object *power*, in each of these cases, should not be confused with one another. As should be clear then, when we use the term *anthropomorphism*, as we have done so above, we are drawing attention to those descriptions of the world which do not originate from beholding nature itself, but instead have origin in descriptions of relations between "man", and their concern with *social power*, as something uniquely exclusive from nature. The anthropomorphism of the *world as power* arises when we explain the natural world according to *social* mechanisms. Such is the case with Schopenhauer, who goes to great lengths to explain the presentation of the world in sociological terms—terms which can be said to have influenced Nietzsche, and his description of *will to power*. However, and even with this in mind, the pervasiveness of this story (namely, of the *world as power*) is unquestionable. Also, we need not even turn towards the imperialism of modern political ideology for evidence. Having been delivered over to the value creation of market economics, which deals with data and statistics for commodifying experiences (and this, for the sake of capital interests), every economic exchange appears to have been rendered into an operation within an economy of social power; whether we are purchasing products or simply hanging the free ones on a Facebook wall, clapping for them on Medium, or liking them on Instagram, and so on. This anthropomorphism of the *world as power* continually forces itself to the foreground of our attention, no matter how much our stomachs may churn, or how much we may want to resist. However, and despite this, what should not be overlooked is precisely the history which we have been following up to this point. This understanding of *the world as dialectic, as will,* or *as power,* has its foundations in *imperium*—command, as the essential ground of *domination as being-superior*, which is only possible as the constant surmounting of others, who are thereby the inferiors. That is to say, this anthropomorphism of *the world as power* is grounded in (what we would call today) *sociologic*. Perhaps it might be helpful to characterize this function of *power*, understood as explanatory of "external" phenomena. In do-

64

ing so, we may even save a bit of Nietzsche's philosophy in the process. Firstly, recall Nietzsche's language of "*slave morality*"; then, secondly, think about such power as belonging to this explanatory *form of life*. While in contrast to that, we have "*master morality*"—a form of life in which we find not the experience of *social power*, but instead, an experience which could be more correctly described as *lust, confidence,* and *euphoria*. Or *envy, anger,* and *fear*. It is these "internal" descriptions which then provide for a projection onto the "external" as power in explanatory sociological terms. The primordial power of what is natural precedes and is prior to even causal explanations, such as those of physics. Now, there should be no doubt that this sociological characterization of the world demands *more* domestication of the human animal, and thereby restricts a readiness for disclosure, truth, and authenticity. Inasmuch, we should be wary of these characterizations. And besides, through our inheritance, we have in our possession institutions which encourage alternatives to *imperium*—and we must admit that those institutions do open up a space in which, at the very least, episteme is suspended. And in these venues, an alternative understanding of power does come to the fore— namely, a power that is, as we have been suggesting, not sociological but *natural*.

Consider, as an example, that which has already been suggested on the very first pages of this opuscule: the art museum. There can be no doubt then, that beyond the curator's self-guiding plaques and those containing the artist's statements, there is a unique space which opens at the art museum—a "safe space" which provides an opportunity for a unique encounter with phenomena. However, we probably want to ask, *does this space negate actio altogether*? After all, when we think of our experience together with the work of art, do we honestly feel that the world is standing still? Actually "no", and this is not what is suggested. But then, we must answer a question for ourselves: *what exactly is released for action?* What primordial *actio*, what pre-intellectual "action", replaces episteme in a work of art? And, possibly closer to the point, can this *actio* inspire a future of healthy economic activity beyond *imperium*?

Inside the safe space of the museum, we not only find a space suitable for reflection; we also find a space where a particular allowance is granted—one which frees us for a complete and utter subjection to the work of art. This allowance is afforded by way of safety and security, such that becoming dominated by the natural power of the artwork is pleasurable. In the vein of philosophical speech and terminology, *the object* is that which comes to "overstand" *the subject*. This is a possibility which, in the social domain, could only be appreciated as a fetish. However, when thinking about the natural domain, and if we allow ourselves to reflect on the most extreme cases, then it is likely that there will be no greater sign of this complete reversal of episteme than the tears which are shed over the phenomena which provoke the experience of the epic. We only need to consider the experience of being captured by Arkhip Ivanovich Kuindzhi's 1880 *Moonlit Night on the Dnieper*, or Maxfield Parrish's 1922 masterpiece, *Romance*. And of course, these examples are not meant to be snooty. This utter subjection found in the encounter with the epic can also be found in the raver who has become entranced by the DJ set. However, this last example may lead us into erroneous thinking. After all, we should keep in mind that an encounter with the aesthetic is not merely sensual. The aesthetic is likewise intellectual. No doubt, ideals and values are animated, alive in the work of art. And what should not be overlooked is that in each case, the objects which present themselves in this space resist quantification. They resist conforming to totality. And even now, if you reflect for just a moment. As this chapter comes to a close, consider your own experience together with this opuscule. It is very likely that part of your enjoyment has come not so much from the factual data or exercises herein, but instead from wandering away from the text itself—off into your own thoughts. Words, phrases, and images from your own experience appear in your mind's eye. While it would be true to say that these objects have been provoked by the opuscule, they are nonetheless no-where to be found within the text itself. No doubt, there is something of a "safe time" which opens up in philosophiz-ing—one which is comparable with the experience during diary reflection, or even cloud watching. In this safe time, there is something of a primordial *actio* mediated by the object—an *actio* which belongs neither to the subject nor to the object. It is this negation of an *I*, in either a subject or an object, which will provide fruitful insights for use in ad-vancing prescriptions for nurturing truth and authenticity in the second half of this work.

 # Fallen Empires

Political sarcasm

Lyrical self-deprecation

Idolization of the apathetic and the cool

What conditions allow for the enjoyment of such aesthetics?

From the vantage point of present time, it is undeniable that the sarcastic themes present in the comedy of George Carlin, John Stewart, and *South Park* have now become transparent. Equally, the self-deprecation of Radio Head and Nine Inch Nails has not aged well. We can say something similar about the apathetic characters of Donn Pearce's *Cool Hand Luke* and Marshall Mathers' Eminem. Undoubtedly, the popularity of the entertainment of the late second millennium indicates a spirit coping with the symptoms of the giantism of the nineteenth and twentieth centuries. The name *postmodernist* has been used to describe these works. However, it must be admitted that this name is only partially appropriate. This aesthetic does not so much celebrate a rejection of the ideals of later modernization, as it does romanticize the suffering from within them. The spirit of postmodernism indicates a deep commitment to the pursuit of industrial-liberation—but at the same time it recognizes that this pursuit had realized in a perversion. Simply consider the idolization of the industrialization of knowledge throughout the scientific industries and journalism, but then also the distrust towards authority, deep state conspiracies, and the appeal of populism. Looking at the early third millennium, we find the appearance of the *conservative skeptic*—one who doubted the coronavirus data that was reported by the mainstream news. We can then assume that this is the same skeptical spirit which took up flat earth theory in order to redeem the value of one's own personal experience. If we say that Gene Roddenberry's *Star Trek* is the most pronounced idolization of modernization, imperial value, and technocratic governance in science fiction, then Chris Carter's *X-Files* must be the postmodern sequel.

Now, what might strike us as peculiar is that this twofold aesthetic periodization—the modern and postmodern—had been prepared for long ago. Already at the inception of the epistemological project during the seventeenth century, Descartes's meditations provide a wealth of material for science fiction novelists of the twentieth. Already then, we can read of a rationalist subjectification of the world coupled with solipsism. No doubt, the insurmountable chasm which opens between the subject, *I*, and the world had prepared for an encounter with the uncanny. This tripartite unfolding of doubt, rationalism, and science fiction may today strike us just as uncanny as the estrangement itself. In recalling Descartes's second meditation, we can remember his reflection as he sat isolated in his apartment,

> "What do I see from my window, but hats and coats which may cover automatic machines? Yet I judge these to be men…"

"And in regard to any corporeal objects, I do not recognize in them anything so great or so excellent that they might not have possibly proceeded from myself…to these it is certainly not necessary that I should attribute any author other than myself…"

These are the words which Descartes writes! Should there be any surprise that maintaining a subjectivist metaphysics, as we have done, has produced an enormous administrative machine engine? From the vantage point afforded to us today, it is hard to imagine any other conclusion to such a Cartesian rationalist subjectification than postmodern suffering. After all, anyone who has come to understand himself as the rationalist metaphysical subject and who, at the same time, idolizes a totalization of the universal powers, will eventually realize that even if this totality could be completed, he would still find himself a mere peripheral within a strange machinery. And anyone who then, at the same time, had come to experience *The Death of God* would find himself alone in a world of cold mechanisms beyond his comprehension—a machinery which had no concern for his interest. And while Kant's epistemological project is said to have improved upon Descartes's, despite all his excruciating detail, we were left without a story of how a metaphysical subject transcends its own subjectivity in order to meet another subject—a story which might bring *a me* into contact with *a you*. Of course, looking into our historical continuum, this solipsism did not go unacknowledged in the years following Kant. However, the problematizing of intersubjectivity had not become explicit until the beginning of the twentieth century. Not until the writing of Edmund Husserl do we find an explicit problematizing of what can be called *intersubjective transcendence*. And still, over the next several decades following Husserl's pronouncement, the problem of intersubjective transcendence went unsolved, such that we inherit it today.

Now, this chapter has been entitled *Fallen Empires*. It is here that our historical narrative of the economy of truth announces the conclusion to episteme. However, the catalyst for this fall should not be confused. Neither subjectivity nor intersubjective transcendence is that which has signaled a confrontation with *episteme*, such that we desire resolution. And in all honesty, if the problems of the primordial *actio* of episteme were merely consequential to intellectualism, then we would not find any reason for economic reform prescriptions. However, we can be sure that this is not the case. After all, it is not by way of Husserl's deliberations that we inherit the epistemological foundations of modernization today. To this we must admit a completely unintellectual source. It is, after all, by way of WWII and the victory of Enlightenment values that we suffer from the symptoms of episteme today. While this claim may be discomforting to those who champion the universal ideal of human rights, at the same time there should be little surprise. There can be no doubt that the name *liberalism* is printed upon every banner of imperialism today. However, if we are to defend such a claim, we must temporarily set aside the historical economy of truth. Of course, a comprehensive understanding of liberalism could only be gained outside the pages of this book, yet a shallow qualification of liberalism is required before we can return to truth—before truth's utility within this project can be made clear. The next few paragraphs will lay bare the project of liberalism as one towards a liberation from governance by way of domestication.

If we look back into the past to the works of Enlightenment philosophers and statesmen, we find a project to liberate the vessel of human potential, the *tabula rasa*—John Locke's *"white paper"*—that blank canvas which is the human subject. Liberalism began as an application of the epistemologist's subject to the domain of governance. The liberation of this subject is promised by way of *rights*. Now, rights themselves exist in many variations—*inalienable rights, natural rights*, and also *human rights*, for example. And while history lessons have a reputation to bore, a history of rights will allow us to emphasize the paradigm of subjectivity, such that we can understand in what form we have inherited episteme, today. Now, what should be noted first, in recounting a history of rights, is that long before Thomas Jefferson penned *The Declaration of Independence* and announced *"inalienable Rights"* (those rights which are characterized by *"Life, Liberty and the pursuit of Happiness"*), these rights—namely, inalienable rights—once referred to a purely metaphysical, or "mental", category—those of internal constitution. Internally, these rights referred to the principle that no matter what earthly rule any man found himself under, his inner world was a realm which was inalienably his own. Consider, as an example of these rights, the story of Christ's forty lashes, as he sat on trial before the Roman governor of Judea, Pontius Pilate. Upon Pilate's interrogation into his kingship, Jesus simply replies, *"my kingdom is not of this world"*. Pilate responds, *"So, you are a king, then!"* To which Jesus retorts, *"You say that I am a king. In fact, the reason I was born and came into the world is to testify to the truth"*. With these words, Jesus qualified the domain of his truth as extraterrestrial. Of course, today, we might find this mere "mental" freedom as a slave's freedom. However, what should be admitted is that as a pre-physical category, these rights were absolutely inalienable. However, within Enlightenment literature, we find that these inalienable rights were transported into the domain of social and material commerce. We could say that the project of

the Enlightenment sought to bring this internal and mental freedom out into the exterior.

Within Enlightenment literature, inalienable rights transformed into something natural. Within Locke's *Second Treatise of Civil Government*, for example, the *state of Nature* refers to that of the individual-subject's primordial commerce. This state is governed by the *law of Nature*, *"which obliges every one, and reason, which is that law,* [that] *no one ought to harm another in his life, health, liberty or possessions* [insofar as each individual is equally independent and equally governed by the law of Nature]*"*. Rights, then, in the writing of Locke, seem to refer to the power which anyone has in this state of Nature. Locke understands these rights exercised by two powers. The first of those powers is to do *"whatsoever he thought fit for the preservation of himself and the rest of mankind"*; the second, *"the power to punish the crimes committed against the law* [of Nature]*"*—and that is to say, the second power is to punish those who violate the preservation of any other individual and the rest of mankind. The project of the Enlightenment sought to safeguard these rights (then appropriately named, *natural rights*) from the violence of the state of Nature, which (again, repeating from John Locke's *Second Treatise of Civil Government*) *"is full of fears and continual dangers"* on account that men are *"biased by their interest, as well as ignorant for want of study of* [their interest], *are not apt to allow of* [the law of Nature] *as a law"*; and that, furthermore, men are partial to themselves and *"passion and revenge carry them too far, and with too much heat in their own cases, as well as negligence and unconcernedness, make them too remiss in other men"*.

As part of the Enlightenment's liberation project, natural rights were to be secured through human reason. Reason was manifest in the commerce of the human animal as *law*.

Locke recognizes in his treatise that every man entering into society with others must give over his power in the state of Nature (as defined above) to the legislative power. Therefore, the first and most fundamental of any law, in the words of Locke, *"is the establishing of the legislative power"* which is to be governed itself by natural law, for *"the preservation of the society and (as far as will consist with the public good) of every person in it"*. The only superior to man was reason, over any king and before any god. The promise of liberation, then, was a **governance as law**, achieved by way of democracy—*a rule of the people.*

In 1802, Thomas Jefferson penned a now historical letter to the Danbury Baptist Association in Connecticut. In this letter, we find the kernel of what would later become a foundational mantra of the liberal project—*the separation of church and state.* When we learn of this separation at a young age, we are likely to think of the hocus-pocus of religion and the powers of governance. The blessing of the tsar by the priest, or the consultation of oracles before going to war. Yet, any primordial reckoning which these fanciful images provoke fades beyond the playground imagination. Even a staunch rejection of such magic signals immaturity. Instead, what calls for such a reckoning today is the function which each half serves within the whole of the dichotomy. We surmise that this functional division must have been clear in Jefferson's mind—a separation of action over-and-above belief,

> "Believing that religion is a matter which lies solely between Man & his God, that he owes account to none other for his faith or his worship, that the legitimate powers of government reach *actions* only, & not *opinions*, I contemplate with sovereign reverence that act of the whole American people which declared that their legislature should 'make no law

> respecting an establishment of religion, or prohibit-
> ing the free exercise thereof', thus building a wall of
> separation between Church & State."

Of course, when looking at our historical records, we understand that the foundation for this wall had been trenched
long before Jefferson's pronouncement; and yet, its popularity signals a utility. Insofar as the legislative power regulates,
curates and develops fair exchanges in the commerce of
"man", Jefferson's separation animates a spirit of mercantilism. This animation is in favor of a form of governance
which, say, animates a community-bodied projection towards the future. Neither does the legislative power animate
other functions within the union of "man"—pronounced
the most are those which the Church meant to satisfy in the
whole of human commerce—namely, *hope, inspiration,* and
communion. Indeed, we find in Jefferson's pronouncement
of a separation between church and state a repetition of
Locke. The purpose of uniting men under a commonwealth
is *"the preservation of their* [commercial liberty and their]
property". However, if we are highly inhuman, we can explain away this liberation as a mere rationalization for the
sake of productivity. After all, from the perspective of productivity, even liberalism is a mere rationalization which
has granted expediency to production—the businessman
being the mere vessel. And in looking at later testimony,
a separation of action over-and-above belief led to a common and widespread critique *against* mercantilism. In 2013,
James Gustave Speth, the United States advisor on climate
change, championed for a spiritual renewal. He warned
of a disintegration of morality from within this economy.
"Greed, selfishness, and apathy" were causing destruction
to nature. Of course today, if we can restrain our feelings
of disgust, we can ask ourselves, *how else was authenticity*

supposed to manifest within market economics? When the value of a product is determined by the market, the individual creator is forced to look towards his activity, his "busyness", as the object of his own value. It is no surprise then that career success would become the barometer for measuring anyone's contribution to his or her people. Plus, in looking at the entertainment industries of the late second millennium, we can find evidence to support this. Friedrich Nietzsche's *"What doesn't kill me, makes me stronger"* came to satisfy that spirit which idolizes individual strength and self-reliance—residue from Enlightenment-era reason and will.

Now, there can be no doubt then that liberalism's mercantilism has announced itself as a preservation of episteme, partly as a result of the effects of the economic policies that took effect following WWII and the Bretton Woods institutions. United States Treasury Secretary Henry Morgenthau stated that the establishment of the International Monetary Fund (IMF) and the International Bank for Reconstruction and Development (IBRD) marked the end of *"economic nationalism"*. Neoliberalism referred to the market-oriented reform policies which eliminated price controls, deregulated capital markets, lowered trade barriers, and reduced state influence, especially through privatization and austerity. Following the collapse of the USSR, we find ourselves resonating with stories which tell of a liberation for a global market, such that the legislative power had become a mere auxiliary. Taking the words of French philosopher Étienne Balibar as testimony from this period, we can now understand that the legislative power had devolved *"from a protective function to a function of destruction of its own civil society"*. A destruction *"not in the 'totalitarian' form, but in the 'utilitarian' form, which is hardly less violent"*. And although these passages are reproduced here by way of his essay, *Our European Incapacity*, it is not hard for us to extend this to any state subjected to federal structures in service to market demands.

Of course, at this point in our historical narrative of rights and liberalism, we should not proceed all-too proudly in thinking that we have singled out our enemy—and that all that is required now is to defeat the libertarians, or the supporters of the United States Republican Party, which favors the selfishness of the rich over the poor, or which values personal wealth and career over the environment. After all, the United States Democratic Party too carries on the tradition of subjectivity—and it does so in a fashion likely more subversive, yet more pronouncedly, than the contemporary libertarian. However, in order to consider this subversive manifestation of subjectivity, we must firstly make explicit what has up to this point only been suggested implicitly—and that is the central role which *"the state of Nature"* comes to serve in determining the essence of liberal politics. Returning again to Locke's *Second Treatise of Civil Government*, it is clear that "man" is naturally a lonesome creature, and that he is naturally separated from other men and, therefore, that their communion is neither in nature, nor natural. The essence of the political, then, as characterized by the Enlightenment, and attested for through this particular piece of Enlightenment literature, is the *"mutual preservation"* of property between individuals. This mutual preservation of property, or *"commonwealth"*, comes with the purpose of securing the ideal of *justice* from the dangers of a savage world. What should not be overlooked is that the legislative power within this commonwealth is concerned with and animates man's domain—this domain, therefore, not only provides for a domestication of nature within that domain, but also a domestication of each other who we equally call "man". However, neither should we overlook the prior condition which is necessary for such a domestication project. What is required is a negative characterization of nature and of the nature of the human animal— perhaps, for example, that the natural state of "man" is as a savage. Through both surveillance and punishment, the liberal project can thus be characterized by overpowering actions—including an overpowering of even one's self. Still today, we hear appeals to the savagery of the world, whether the purpose of this appeal is to encourage the necessary protection of one's property (this is a popular appeal within contemporary discussions on the right to bear arms, for example), or for appealing to a virtuous self-sacrifice for "the benefit of the greater good". We should not be mistaken; liberalism has, since its inception, problematized savagery.

Now, there can be no denying that domestication, today, is no longer solely conducted by way of an administrative legislative power, including law, surveillance, and punishment, but is also supplanted with social justice activism. In expanding upon and redefining the subject of liberalism's rights (which, according to the contemporary Left market narrative, is no longer the individual-subject, but is instead the gender, race, or sexually-orientated identity group), social justice activism carries on liberalism's project of domestication. While this is perhaps a shocking claim to those who champion for human rights, if we are honest with ourselves, then Black Lives Matter, feminist activism, and LGBTQ+ activism, while perhaps founded upon productive intentions, do maintain a character of law, surveillance, and punishment. What should not be overlooked is that each of these political movements are only possible from a position of liberalism's problematizing savagery. Each must animate savagery, each in their own respective fields of interest, in order to retain power. Now, because of this fork in the understanding of the *subject* of rights, our historical narrative must make use of a more articulated language. Therefore, as we go forward, we will draw further distinctions and designate the subject of epistemological metaphysics and of classical liberalism as *the individual-subject*. If we must refer to the social activist's identity group subject, we will use the name *identity-subject*.

Equally relevant to this narrative of the identity-subject is the extension of this social governance into the private spheres by way of the markets. No doubt, liberal governance had established a foundation for a much more nuanced domestication of the human animal than what could have been possible through democratic infrastructure alone. This was accomplished by way of applying public pressure to marketing narratives. Inasmuch, private businesses were able to satisfy public interests more than any government institution. This narrative is evident as demonstrated in the aftermath of the death of George Floyd. However, what becomes plainly obvious then, when presented with extensions of *governance as law* to the private market, is that liberalism had not so much defeated tyranny—whether that of authoritarianism or its fascist manifestations. Instead, by way of shame and virtue signaling, the primordial *actio* of overstanding is preserved. Of course, while this narrative holds a natural power over us today, we should also admit that in defaulting the preservation of episteme to liberalism, we are not also saying that liberal governance was not the better of the options at the close of WWII—than say, the planned economy of the Soviets, or the state imperial machine of Nazi Germany—but that, after all, liberalism's market economy is that by which episteme survives, such that we suffer from it today. Inasmuch, we should not be surprised to find champions for liberation going under the banner of *nationalism*. After all, even if it is regressive rather than progressive, nationalism offers many supporters a great deal of refuge from the markets. It calls back to a time when there were *nations of people*; when proximal communities still made sense. Yet, regarding nationalism, we must ask ourselves an honest question: *can patriotism jive with our project to nurture truth and authenticity?* We have already admitted that estrangement is pronounced in the revenge of the post-colonial narratives and in social justice activism; but estrangement is equally pronounced in the reaction-ary masculinist movements, and in calls for the founding of ethnostates. We are pitted against each other—neighbor against neighbor, friend against friend, and relative against relative. Can there be any doubt that such a state of affairs obscures the possibility for genuine authenticity?

Standing here in this very moment, the conclusions of epis-teme, as the guiding *actio* of modernization, have become transparent. Episteme lays itself bare for everyone to see. The liminal *here* and *now* of today is characterized by the very identification of this narrative. A question. Can anyone bear this visage? Who among us could continue down this path—idolizing doubt, problematizing savagery (including a savagery in one another) and idolizing the true and the false of *imperium's* domination? This opuscule is for those who are inspired to reconcile with this history. From this position, we then find the emergence of a new project for the future. The completion of this project could only be sig-naled after a resolution to the alienation, rootlessness, es-trangement, and apathy which we have inherited by way of the imperialism, totalitarianism, universalism, and giantism of episteme. This project is beyond the post-colonial narratives, the residual after-effects of patriarchy, and the suffering of the postmodern aesthetic outright. Of course, this work is just one component in this initiative, and it is guided by merely two objects, truth and authenticity. Yet, these two objects are of paramount importance to the completion of this project. Nurturing either requires laying a foundation, and this foundation requires, firstly, that we redeem truth from the epistemological paradigm, such that the locus of value creation, authenticity itself, may be liberated. This task alone defines this work.

The Liberal Solution, Metamodernism

We have now come to understand the essential economy in which truth is in service to—that which we have identified as *parse to transcend*. In turn, we have identified the primordial *actio* and comportment towards the world by which this essence has been expedited: *episteme*. We are, therefore, allowed to return to our object *truth*. We must now trace the path that truth followed through the post-WWII narrative presented in the previous chapter. In doing so, we will have completed the first half of this opuscule. And while the reader may be eager for an identification and description of an economic alternative to episteme, specifically as manifest within capitalism and market economics, this concluding chapter is still necessary. After all, it is precisely by way of a confidence in liberal values that we confront the seeming absolutism of *epistemological relativism*—a "worldview" at odds with our orgasmic, sensual, and ecstatic experience of truth. This chapter will introduce *metamodernism*, a political discussion that arose during the post-WWII period. In taking up the metamodern narrative into our own narrative here, we will be able to approach epistemological relativism by way of what has been called *the problematizing of cri-*

tique. And, in confronting the problem of epistemological relativism politically, we will find peace with our liberation from governance. With such peace, it will become apparent that continuing with the pursuit of the Enlightenment—namely, to place reason over any king and before any god—is now an irrelevant project. Of course, given what has been explicated in the previous chapters, it should be clear that when speaking of *liberalism*, we are not treating of the political narratives of Left and Right—where one could be "financially conservative" and "socially progressive". We are referring to either position along either axis within liberal governance. And after all, from the vantage point *here*, the financial and social have collapsed onto a singular line. In order to promote financial liberalism, we must also accept social liberalism. The market demands it.

If we then turn our attention to the intellectual debate following WWII, we find a prioritization of disarming and disempowering world institutions—even those far beyond the reach of the Nuremberg trials. The intellectuals who deconstructed authority during this period enjoyed the prestige of public celebrity. These thinkers were burdened with the task of reconciling with that causal-occult and sociological object *power* which had been inherited by way of Hegel, Marx, Schopenhauer, and Nietzsche. We can epitomize this period by referencing the debate surrounding intellectuals such as Hans-Georg Gadamer, Jürgen Habermas, and Jacques Derrida, among others. In a little-referenced academic paper from 2003, titled *The Problem of Critique*, Steven M. Feldman identifies this turn away from epistemological metaphysics and towards a certain *epistemological sociology*, one that goes by the name of *metamodernism*,

> "Metamodernism not only rejects epistemological foundationalism, but further dismisses these con-

cerns as insignificant in comparison to other more pressing issues. Metamodernists tend to emphasize the operation and orientation of power."

"Jürgen Habermas, for instance, unequivocally declares himself to be postmetaphysical."

However, this turn towards the deconstruction of authority was not entirely healthy for liberalism. After all, as part of the deconstruction, we find a commitment to abandoning epistemological fundamentalism—an idea ushered in by way of Heidegger. In its place, Gadamer, for example, adopted something of a socially conditioned understanding of the individual-subject—a social condition he called *"tradition"*. However, in abandoning the sole accountability of the epistemologist's individual-subject, these metamodernists found themselves in the middle of a paradox. Feldman framed this paradox as *the problematizing of critique within the metamodern paradigm.* That is,

"If we are always situated in a communal or cultural context, then how can we criticize either a particular interpretation of a text or, more broadly, a societal arrangement or organization?"

And if there is no *objective ruler of the standard* for societal arrangement, then *"metamodernism problematizes critique"* instead. And this problem *"leads us into the political conundrum"*. But what exactly is this political conundrum which Feldman announces?—well, nothing other than the political problem of epistemological relativism—or rather, perhaps more simply, *relativism.* If every local world narrative is conditioned by a tradition that is beyond anyone's accountability, then how do we responsibly justify critique?

In a rapidly globalizing economy, on what foundation can world leaders justify their actions over others?

Now, simply because of its pervasiveness, this question may appear to be either the most trivial or the most dire problem which could be encountered. And yet, what should not be mistaken is that, in either case, it is not the intellect which decides for or against the value of such a problem. The value could only be measured in terms of the reckoning which the problem provokes. Let us not forget that the writing of the metamodernists is a testament to the suffering which this problem has caused—and to that list of thinkers, we can also include the American philosopher of science, Karl Popper, who had perversely attempted to justify *intolerance* for the sake of liberalism. Feldman's announcement only encourages a confrontation with the political problematizing of critique once again. Of course, it should also be said that while the problem opens up a space for such dire considerations as the future of liberal governance, we should also hold a bias towards the most viable solutions. It is, therefore, to the most viable ways forward that we should now turn our attention to.

The problem of critique can be said to have been answered roughly fifteen years following Feldman's announcement. It is here that we find metamodernism fully realized as a political movement. In 2017, Emil Ejner Friis and Daniel Görtz's Scandinavian school of political metamodernism continued the sociological tradition, mostly by way of adult development theorists such as Ken Wilber, Michael Commons, Don Beck, and Chris Cowan, among others. Their book, *The Listening Society*, addresses the problems of liberalism explicitly; inasmuch, they implicitly address the problematizing of critique. Their solution?—what could be called *social value periodization*. Within the language taken up in *The Listen-*

ing Society, we can find an abandonment of epistemological fundamentalism, as well as an appropriation of Nietzsche's value thinking. The Scandinavians understand that human animals throughout the ages have all met each other with common challenges. Those challenges, then, are something of a social challenge. In response, social values, or social value systems, are realized in order to mobilize solutions. Looking through the history of modernization, we find that these social values can be mapped out as a progressive journey—one which facilitates modernization itself. After all, social value systems which mobilize a people to overcome their challenges are healthy; however, those same values are unhealthy if they retard solutions to the next generation's challenges. Of all the world's value systems, metamodern values are the most progressive, having succeeded both the modern and the postmodern—which themselves have succeeded the "Faustian values" of pre-modern times, and so on. Equipped with such a social development theory, we can critique any particular local world narrative and, at the same time, affirm it as one piece of a developmental journey towards globalization.

Of course, the Scandinavians are also keenly aware that in announcing "the global", they not only encourage activities which lead us towards *the empire*, but they also idolize that end goal as well. So, how have they resolved this in good conscience? By way of an appropriation of Nietzsche's value thinking into sociology, the Scandianvians take up two objects for reconciling with their apparent imperialism—both *overman* and *aristocracy*, namely. The Scandinavians understand that the ethical is not some value held by anyone in particular, and certainly not themselves, but is held instead by a "society", or perhaps even the *zeitgeist*. Hanzi Freinacht is the fictitious omniscient world observer and author of political metamodernist literature. As a *no one*, he is an *any one of us*. He represents the *zeitgeist*. He is the "metamodern overman". This literary device apparently allows the Scandinavians to escape *imperium* and, at the same time, assert their metamodern value. Of course, what should be noted is that in adopting this literary device, they have forfeit ownership of even their own ethics, whether explicitly or not, over to an independent and third-party *ruler*. This device allows the Scandinavians to remain scientific and "objective" sociologists. Yet, at the same time, and speaking in psychological terms, we can say that the Scandinavians have also *projected their ethics* onto society as *the moral*. The ethical is then tantamount to the moral. However, we should not forget that this type of psychological projection is a move which has been called *nihilistic* by some (consider the writing of Arthur van den Bruck, for example) and called by others a perverse animation of social morale over the ethical. Of course, the second of these critiques has the possibility of seeming quite pedantic. After all, the social morale and someone's personal ethics may align quite well. And in such a case, the difference may be quite insignificant. In this case, resistance to "mob rule" has no meaning. So then, we must ask, *what is the actual content of the Scandinavian metamodernists' combined ethics and social morale?* Of primary importance are global climate change, animal rights, and the psychological welfare of the human animal. In their political program, these challenges require an appropriation of many worldviews—or, in the language of Nietzsche, many *perspectives*. It is by *listening* that you *gain perspective*. And therefore, in their words, *"those with the most perspectives win"*. Then, having been equipped with a multi-perspective backpack, it is a *metamodern aristocracy* which is to be responsible for holding the world's hand and guiding it towards global governance.

No doubt, one of the most affirmative qualities of the meta-modern narrative is that it announces an end to the suffer-ing of the postmodern aesthetic. Furthermore, for those of us seeking to nurture truth and authenticity, we find ourselves sympathetic to the program of the Scandinavian metamodernists. After all, without any further explication, we can immediately see that *listening* is in some way related to *the disclosure of truth*. Yet, at the same time, we do feel some degree of hesitation towards this political program. After all, we must admit that any idolization of listening in service to *"winning"* is quite perverse. Furthermore, it must be admitted that while having a diverse backpack full of per-spectives is an intrinsic good, what cannot be overlooked is the equally destructive consequences. Any appropriation of "outsider" perspectives does not simply add on to one's per-spective backpack; it also destroys the previous perspective in equal measure. There is no genuine "multi-perspectiv-al" view of the world. There can only ever be one perspec-tive—"one's worldview". And here, it might be wiser to take heed of Martin Luther King Jr.'s critique of the epistemolog-ical project, its totalitarianism and its imperialism, when he remarked in his autobiography that from within Hegel's *"exposition of the coming to be of knowledge"*, absolute ideal-ism *"swallows the many in the one"*. It seems a confusion to champion for epistemic imperialism, and at the same time, champion a readiness for the disclosure of truth.

Of course, whether such a destruction of perspective is healthy depends entirely on the project which we find our-selves in. And perhaps our unique position today, living in the anthropocene—that period in which the human animal is, for the first time, causing negative consequences to the earth's geological substrate—requires a globally coordinated project. Perhaps now the earth itself demands metamodern values from us! Therefore, despite such dramatic claims of conquest and domestication on behalf of metamodernism, we must also acknowledge that submitting the unique perspective to uniform progress may prove to be the correct move. Perhaps we should not seek unique disclosure? After all, if we understand that the global crises are, in fact, the crises of the future, then our efforts today (if they are going to have any meaning whatsoever) must mobilize a globally coordinated project. What should be considered then is whether or not we believe that "the global" narrative is that which will inspire solutions in the emergent project—namely solutions to alienation, rootlessness, estrangement, and apathy. These are, after all, the very obstacles which the metamodern aristocracy would face when coordinating their global project.

Therefore, to consider this further, let us now take up a higher vantage point on which to frame the antagonism which we have been considering up to this point, but have not yet made explicit—that which lies between *truth* and *progress*. After all, what must be plainly obvious is that the social value progressivism of the Scandinavian metamodernists does not so much solve the relativity of truth; rather, *progress* is esteemed as the third-party *ruler* by which we measure truth. It could be said that truth, in the metamodern narrative, is subjected to something of *a teleological relativism*; this has not escaped the Scandinavians, and they admit as much. Metamodern truths are not the final stop. Those truths are provisional, merely *the best we have so far*. However, what must be obvious, especially to anyone who has considered this antagonism with any amount of penetration, is that neither the project of modernization nor globalization are cosmic forces of nature. Therefore, we only require a bit of our metaphysical architectonic in order to resolve the antagonism between truth and progress. First-ly, the future is not some metaphysical destiny which plays with social values as its tool for actualization. Of course, this is not some profound metaphysical claim. It simply means that if there was no primordial discourse (that which is a condition for the articulation of the world)—a discourse between every human animal, non-human animal, and ma-chine, along with every other experiential phenomenon—then *progress* could not be articulated. The evidence for this condition is the very appearance of the world itself. Since without it, no common activity could be made to effectively contend with the world, such that the world could be artic-ulated as the world that it is. We would have no successful discourse—no successful language. Without which, as the biologist might say, *our species would have died out long ago*. In placing discourse in its proper place within the meta-physical architectonic, as *the condition for progress* (or as that which precedes progress), then truth, as that which is produced by discourse, is released from the *imperium* of the metamodernist. Progress is a result of truth, not the other way around. Inasmuch, if we must speak of any substantial "progress" at all, then it can only be as an epiphenomenon. And once we drop the pretense, shame and virtue signaling, it then becomes clear that our ideal of ecological sustainabil-ity could never be accomplished by way of domestication at the hands of a metamodern aristocracy anyway—even if each of us belonged to that aristocracy, and if the domes-tication manifested as pure self-discipline. A self-sacrifice.

On this point, we should not cast aside too quickly our aversion to *sacrifice* and stories which appeal to "the greater good", for the sake of "the global", or "humanity". Because the nature of language is to draw contrast, and thus for the sake of a more articulated commerce, these ideals fight against the very nature of language. Inasmuch, any object which we might come to think of as "the global" (or any "oneness" whatsoever) could only be that primordial *wheeling and dealing with nature*—that pre-linguistic, pre-intellectual or pre-cognitive discourse, which is the very condition for any articulation of the world, and includes not only the commerce of the human animal, but also every element of the earth. If we allow ourselves a bit of honesty, then it becomes clear that our ideal of ecological sustainability could only be satisfied by way of a robust and harmonious symbiosis with nature; thus, neither self-disciplining nor sacrificing could ever be possible. If we return the human animal to nature, *then when you nurture "man", you also nurture nature,* and *vice versa.* Inasmuch, we cannot assume any higher type of man—an overman—who stands in relationship to those "men" below him. A return to value maintenance by way of Nietzsche's master-slave dialectic (if interpreted sociologically) must today strike us as regressive—even if that dialectic is maintained by way of a fantastic *every one/no one*, like Hanzi Freinacht, "society", or by the global metamodern aristocracy. Therefore, if we take up the language of the overman at all, then it must be as a goal. *"Not man, but overman is the goal"*, says Nietzsche. This goal does not belong to the category "man" as a type of *superman*, but could only be achieved by being beyond *the object "man" as an object to be reckoned with.* Once we are over "man", once that designation *no longer makes sense* as a metaphysical category and remains, as it is, merely as a physical description of the male-gendered human animal, then and only then will the overman have inherited the earth. Finally, in animating the domain of nature, we are allowed to animate exactly that which the Scandinavians have so blatantly obscured when they hid behind their fictitious author, Hanzi Freinacht—namely, perspective, truth, and authenticity. The Scandinavians are not *meta*modern enough.

Of course, in submitting ourselves to this aversion to sacrifice and to perspective, let it be clear that we are not also forfeiting ourselves to the unfortunate reality of the selfishness of the human animal. Instead, we repel that narrative too. This accounts for why we find suspicion towards Greta Thunberg, both to her narrative and her popularity, among many of our contemporaries. Stories of punishment such as Greta's animates the selfishness of the human animal over perspective. Once we find ourselves at the closing of this opuscule, and if at that moment we do decide to advance towards prescriptions for nurturing the disclosure of truth, then we should beware of this common *problematizing of perspective*. What will be required of us in the emergent project is to eventually forgo the language of "perspective" altogether. Until then, we must allow for talk of perspective, but only as a type of transitional, or perhaps educational, language. Such transitional and educational language would then make use of perspective in order to direct the student to the "objective" domain, to nature, and to the phenomena themselves, as those phenomena present themselves over to *a you* and *a me*.

However, for those who may be on the fence, and who resonate with a continued animation of man's domain and of man's domination over nature, perhaps on account of the global existential crises of climate change, we can refer to a book written in 1970—a rather biblical text by E.F. Schumacher, titled *Small is Beautiful*. To this day, it remains relevant not only for answering questions related to commodification and market economics, but also for addressing the symptoms of industrialization in general. At the height of its influence, this book became a cornerstone of Green Movement literature. There can be no doubt then, that laying behind the printed words of that text, we can read of a spirit championing for a complete reversal of episteme. Inasmuch, this opuscule, *How to Nurture Truth and Authenticity*, could correctly be billed as something of a sequel—one which is now fifty years overdue. Therefore, it is only fitting that the second half of this work be introduced by repeating a few passages—ones which should be kept in mind as we come closer to our prescriptions for economic reform,

> "Instead of overcoming the 'world' by moving towards salientness, man tries to overcome it by gaining preeminent wealth, power, science, or indeed any imaginable 'sport'...He is driven to build up a monster economy and to seek fantastic satisfaction, like landing on the moon...This economy of giantism is a left-over of nineteenth-century conditions and nineteenth-century thinking and it is totally incapable of solving any of the real problems of today."

> "An entirely new system of thought is needed, a system based on attention to people, and not primarily attention to goods...and what was neglected in the nineteenth century is unbelievably urgent now. That is, the conscious utilisation of our enormous technological and scientific potential for the fight against misery and human degradation—a fight in intimate contact with actual people, with individuals, families, small groups, rather than states and other anonymous abstractions. This presupposes a political and organizational structure that can provide this intimacy."

As we go forward into the second half of this work, let us keep in our hearts that final word—*"intimacy"*.

What is now required by the second half of this work is, firstly, an understanding of truth which can ground an infrastructure providing for authenticity. To do so, we must turn towards a foundation prior to doubt, prior to the demand for certainty, and prior to the positive fact outright—and this is not meant as an aggrandizement. The framework we are moving into is *a priori*. If we are to nurture truth and authenticity in the emergent project, then we must not merely replace *epistemological fundamentalism* with *epistemological sociology* and thereby continue within an economy of *imperium's* domination.

Instead, we must get behind epistemological fundamentalism. This means we must return to the conditions of possibility. In the second half of this opuscule we will construct an architectonic of those conditions by way of our object truth. This architectonic will help us to describe that very process of a *wheeling and dealing discourse with nature* which we have referenced throughout this development—that which is the condition for the very appearance of the world. Construction of this framework will name a primordial *actio*, counter to that of episteme and it will, furthermore, allow us to reconstitute subjectivity such that we can move into political activity beyond either liberalism's individual-subject or identity-subject. We will, after all, walk away with a new subject in the second half of this work and, therefore, a new form of subjectivity. However, in order to proceed with this architectonic, we must allow ourselves to come back to the "less pressing" issue of the epistemological sociologists, to metaphysics—in particular we will begin with a phenomenological method of inquiry. This method of inquiry will offer us insights for materializing the prophecies of *Small is Beautiful*. Only from phenomenological methodology can we resolve the feeling that life is becoming more and more complex, and that we require more sophisticated forms of data processing to render this complexity manageable. In the second half of this work, we will meet with the aesthetic experience of *the beautiful*—an aesthetic which presences once we remove the unnecessary and superfluous. A beauty which accompanies simplicity by way of logic's ability to "*release complexity*" from the world (Bonnitta Roy), such that affectivity can be animated. A beauty which Schumacher captured in the word *small*.

SECOND HALF

Truth for
an Emergent Project

Following all that has come before, we can now say with confidence that today, truth is subservient to *imperium*—the command. And for us, living *here* and *now*, it is hard to imagine anything besides that. Nearly all phenomena of experience conform to that anthropomorphism of *the world as power*. An idolization of liberal values, specifically those which have guided us towards liberation, has perversely animated the social power substrate. Yet, despite a feeling of estrangement from the aims of the Enlightenment, this does not mean that we are without an inheritance passed down to us from that time period. Already by 1962, Hans-Georg Gadamer had identified that the romanticism of the eighteenth century began with a total estrangement from tradition. One hundred years later, having defeated the first wave of challengers to liberal machination during WWII, the spirit of romanticism announced itself for a third time—in this instance, it was mostly and noticeably more pronounced within the social revolutionary movements of the 1960s and 1970s. We can be sure, then, that romantic aesthetics will surface time and time again, whether through conservation or progress, wherever we find the smog of industrial-liberation. The emergent project demands the same kinds of animative force found in the breath of creation. Of paramount value are both the individual's affectivity in the process of creating the world image, and secondly, a reunion of life and work that are then taken as a whole. Therefore, this project, including the contribution of this opuscule, unquestionably manifests this spirit of romanticism.

Fixed as we are, we find a particular demand from truth itself: to be delivered from dialectic, will, and power. This means that truth demands to be delivered from the logic of society and its subsequent relativism. Our project to nurture truth and authenticity requires that we return to truth's conditioning in the primordial harmony with nature. Truth demands that our project be in possession of *reality*—satisfying our want for a truth in accordance with *the real*. After all, if we are honest with ourselves, there can be no doubt as to the reality of our world. The evidence for such reality is the very appearance of the world. If there was no reality to this world, then no activity could be made to effectively contend with it. We would have no successful discourse—no successful language. This holds whether you live in a world described by the incomplete explanations of the Big Bang, or whether you go further with a more comprehensive language of God. Consider that even in denouncing religion, you are still a creation of God, *are you not?* Because for a Christian, you surely are; this should be no surprise. It is the nature of the world that we all live in the same world, together—no matter if, whether or not, our world is solely described by physics, or if supplanted with the occult objects of the Christian doctrine. We can say that we live in a world which is both intimate, yet also the largest thing that is comprehensible to us.

Now, this chapter is primarily definitional. The next few pages will identify the economy in which the Anglo-Germanic *truth* found service prior to its Latinization. This chapter will consider both **description** and **judgement**, before finally affirming the nature of truth as **disclosive** and **projective**. All of this will then join up with that which has been qualified in the previous chapters. Specifically, we will make use of *ομοιωσις* (*homoiosis*, "the disclosive correspondence expressing the unconcealed") which presences *λογος* (*logos*), such that the phenomena of experience come into accord with one another. Together, these objects will be used for the construction of a metaphysical architectonic. This architectonic will be used in the identification of a primordial *actio*—that which will be appropriately named *αληθευειν* (*alētheuein*, "to adhere to the unconcealed disclosive in the saying that lets appear"). This *actio*, *αληθευειν*, will then be contrasted against *episteme* in order to guide our prescriptions for nurturing truth and authenticity in the emergent project. What should be kept in mind is that our affirmation of truth as disclosive and projective will not dispose of truth as the positive fact, but will instead situate the factual category of truth within a larger whole.

Here, at the outset of the aforementioned architectonic, we now address the first definition by way of a question, *what is this "disclosive" and "projective" nature of truth?* First of all, we should not be so eager for an answer that we risk not allowing ourselves an opportunity to consider a helpful and relevant exercise—one which might provide for an embodied understanding of disclosure and projection.

If you take a look around you—"yes" at the very location in which you are reading this book—then imagine a freeze-framed snapshot of this location. Imagine that a project had been funded with the peculiar aim of documenting everything within this singular moment. Let us say that this project has already reached its completion. It produced not only the documentation of the color, size, and shape of every humanly visible object occupying this location, but it also documented their compositional properties—exhausted, not with such descriptions as *wood*, *ceramic*, and *concrete*, but with their atomic properties also. And since this project sought to document everything, this resulted in the recorded information of trillions of particles and waves, failing to satisfy the project's conclusive endings. Let us say that you (the discoverer of this project's documentation) also found that the relational properties such as the distances between particles had been measured as well. Furthermore, this project noted hypothetical properties too, such as the color of objects at different times of the day, or the sounds produced when certain objects struck others. This "raw" information (perhaps defined as information without purpose—"pure information") was then analyzed and ordered into different schemes, such that its volume surpassed that of all the information available on the internet. However, despite the apparent logical consistency and experimental rigor taken in producing this information, you would still have a hard time admitting that any one piece of it was true. After all, you would have no feeling of either its truth or its falsehood. And to produce such a feeling in yourself would require the verification of its data—experiencing the phenomena for yourself. And yet, sitting alone with this document, the question would undoubtedly arise, *why would you undertake such excruciating procedures in order to have the truth?* Well, let us be honest, you would undertake this only if having the truth of that information set was relevant—only if it had a consequence on your life.

Beyond this quite fantastical imagery, we can come away with a rather simple confirmation of a long-told story. We can at least go back as far as 1873, to Friedrich Nietzsche's *On Truth and Lying In A Non-moral Sense*. "*Human beings are indifferent to pure knowledge if it has no consequence*"—and we find this to be true even for the positive fact. However, as such, we are presented with quite a peculiar revelation. Having the truth is dependent on consequence, and we can be certain of this conclusion despite the concern lurking within—namely, the concern that truth can only be such on account of an *author* of that truth who understands it as such. Of course, these conclusions direct our thoughts to the very question at hand regarding the nature of truth—a nature which seems to be conditioned by *subjectivity*. This immediately brings into question the relativity of truth. However, we should not be too hasty; let us restrain ourselves from burdening subjectivity with relativism. After all, we have yet to be shown the consequences of such a "subjectification" of the world. Let it be noted that we have renounced both the *individual-subject* and the *identity-subject* in the first half of this opuscule; yet, we have not renounced subjectivity outright. So far, our development has not yet provided an opportunity to define subjectivity—and what should be obvious is that we have not yet even properly delineated *the subject* of this opuscule! However, not to worry, for we will define our subject over the course of the next two chapters, once we have properly delineated truth here in this chapter.

Now, despite the apparent relativism in understanding the true as the consequent, there is also something positive to be gained from thinking about the phenomenal experience of life as a condition for the possibility of truth. What should not be overlooked is how the word *author* has been intentionally used. There is something revealing about the nature of truth in authorship—something which, quite unexpectedly, points towards a certain primordial condition for the possibility of truth. Looking back at recorded testimony from artists throughout the ages, we find evidence of this primordial condition prior to any author—one which instructs and directs all authors. We can find one example of this with the British poet and printmaker William Blake for instance, who attested to being subjected to (and influenced by) sources outside of himself. Of course, having grown up exposed to certain occult figures found in Christian mythology, we should not be surprised to read that Blake's instructor came to him in the form of Biblical archangels. Similarly, we have Mozart's testimony too, where he also said that *"he didn't feel like a composer as much as an* amanuensis, *someone taking dictation from a source outside the self"* (a passage borrowed here from Diana Fosha's *The Healing Power of Emotion*). This subjection of the author to his world is not limited to the painter, poet, nor composer. We must also acknowledge that authenticity manifests in each and every one of us. Even that glorified metaphysical object of the epistemologists, *reason*, serves as the creative faculty of "man"—only narrowly from the domain of the logical-mathematical. And if we take a moment to reflect on those who demand our admiration, like those venerable grandparents of ours who stood like pillars of kindness and wisdom throughout our childhoods, we find that their behavior points towards a common understanding—that any individual is forever subjected to his or her own innermost phenomenal experience. Love, admiration, and forgiveness are not decisions which anyone takes. Instead, they are descriptions of dispositions which the author of those objects finds himself in. This insight allows for the resoluteness which we find in maturity. Without this kind of understanding, any author of, say, forgiveness for example, will misunderstand the reasons why he should be commended for having forgiven in the first place. And yet, exercising forgiveness is admirable—and this is on account of what it signals; that the author has in his possession something of a pre-intellectual reconciliation, or a trophy for having reconciled with his experiences.

This subjection of the author to even his own-most dispositions is not reserved for the judgement of friends, colleagues, or lovers—or any other object or event. This utter subjection to the phenomenal experience also extends to truth. Simply consider an experience in which one *comes to the truth*. Consider the possibility that two or more rationalized "fantasies" are being explored. One observes how the fantasy strikes them—but they are still and always subjected to their nature. No one can simply decide to have one feeling about a fantasy over another. This exercise can be said to describe the jury member's psychological process of judgement, as he is presented with evidence by the attorneys. At the same time, this exercise can equally describe the scientist's psychology, as he is guided by one form of logic or another. Of course, this conclusion (that an author is both solely accountable for their judgement, as the author and "location" of that judgement, yet is completely subjected to the truth of any one description of the world) is likely to cause a certain kind of heartache for some. Think of the age-old maxims dispensed as relationship advice. You cannot help the feelings that you have; you simply have them— well, until you don't. But you should not have to apologize for having those feelings. And what is more, you should not make someone else feel bad for having them, either. There is something of a *paradox of accountability* regarding the judgement of truth. An acknowledgement of this paradox signals one of the great conclusions which will have to be reckoned with as we transition into the emergent project; namely, that any one of us must suffer from our own-most personal judgements—judgements which an *I* alone is capable of producing. Insofar as an author simply finds himself in possession of his own judgement, our prescriptions for nurturing authenticity must forgo any bitterness which we may hold towards that which has been called "subjectivity" since after the writings of Kant. Only by looking at the phenomenal experience of the world can truth escape relativity and remain what it is—an articulation of objects founded upon a primordial discourse with nature. Then, once the phenomena are articulated as an object, any author must immediately acknowledge the instruction which the phenomena have dictated to him. Inasmuch, we absolve ourselves of any "selfishness" resulting from our subjection to the phenomenal experience. Instead, we take up phenomenology as a virtue, and this must mean to us something like so: a commitment to the phenomena as they appear, of themselves, as the objects which they are. Both phenomena and objects are, by their very constitution, *natural* and *naturally occurring.*

Now, what is likely to be pronounced for any highly attuned readers is that in order to bring to light this pronounced *subjection to the truth*, we have made use of *psychologic* and borrowed language from psychology—for example, we have made use of *description, judgement,* and *authenticity.* This has been done on account of the familiarity of this way of reasoning. Not to be mistaken, psychology has revolutionized the way in which we communicate our "internal" experience of the world—and that is to say, the logic of the psyche *has been* helpful within the project of modernization, thus far. Furthermore, many modern philosophers have understood that reasoning through psychologic and with psychological objects proves to be a good foundation for communicating a description of the primordial conditions of possibility. However, if we are to work ourselves out of episteme and into using terms based around a new kind of subjectivity, then we must eventually work ourselves out of the individual-subject of this science. Specifically, regarding our own project, we must eventually use the reasoning of psychologic and psychological objects for establishing a new subject and an architectonic of *first economics* philosophy. To begin this project, let us think back to the second chapter of this opuscule. In doing so, we remember our analysis of projection. We also remember that *projection* is best expressed figuratively or by way of analogy. Consider again the previously offered examples: hunger or sexual desire. Hunger is a condition which not only precedes eating, but also precedes any encountering of food, whatsoever. Sexual desire not merely precedes sexual intercourse, it also precedes identification of the sexes, such that we may have genders to speak of at all. However, and again, we should not get caught up in the analogies. Projection conditions an orientation towards the future in its most robust sense—it conditions descriptions which provide for that future. *The good* or *the just* are descriptions which provide for a realization of goodness or justice in the future. Therefore, we can borrow from the psychological toolkit and say that projection has a "judgemental" character about it. However, if we were to take up a less psychological language, then we would simply say that the quality of *being projective* is that by which any one description can "prove" its truth. And to explicitly announce the conclusion of this argument, we say that *truth is projective in its very nature*. Yet, with this conclusion, let us also repeat once again how we have not yet made explicit the subject of our opuscule. At most, let us only say that any author, as the "location" or locus of authenticity (and one who is also subjected to the truth of any one description), is necessarily subjected to the subject of our opuscule. Therefore, "judgement", if we could speak of it at all, and especially in terms of *first economics* philosophy, belongs to *our* subject.

Of course, as has been promised, this understanding of the nature of truth does not dispose of truth as *the positive fact*. Instead, such a definition allows us to situate *the fact* within the larger whole of truth and thereby affirm it afresh. Here is how that affirmation follows: any description which either fails or is simply too poor at describing the world (which is more often the case), or if that description proves itself as an obstructive (whether as a mechanical and cause-and-effect obstruction, or as a social obstruction), then that particular description equally fails the "test" of truth. It fails to be projective and therefore fails *to be true* of the world. In such cases, that description shows itself to be either *yet to be decided on,* or as conclusively *false*. Of course, for those who are scientifically minded, it may seem like our qualification has done nothing to modify the nature of truth, and that we should simply (as we have always done) toss aside "subjective" worldviews which are no longer projective within the scientific project—such as those descriptions offered by the various religions. Yet, what should be obvious, given that the positive fact is *merely* one type of projective truth among many other possibilities, is that *the false* only becomes a possibility in narrow cases. Inasmuch, the often-praised *falsifiability* proves to be inessential in regards to the judgement of truth. Now, not to be mistaken, truth is *worldly*, even in our definition put forward here. The world, by its own very definition, is common to everyone; therefore, what should be noted is that claims to the existence of the causal-occult, such as the existence of God, cannot be proven true or false in any scientific sense. Such an "existence" could only be proven in the soul, so to speak. What remains outstanding, then, regarding our qualification of the nature of truth as *projective*, are the consequences to projection when leaving descriptions such as "God" *yet to be decided on* (if, of course, we find that description to be as yet undecided). Furthermore, what should be noted about this matter is that we have hardly even begun our approach towards a description of "the venue" and "the forum" where "the event" and the judgement of truth can be found. And for now, our apparent promotion of a lifestyle full of worldly and common truths, yet with a pronounced *lack of decision* on seemingly dire matters, will have to be discussed in a later chapter.

Concluding our definition, and if we return to the etymology of truth as introduced in previous chapters, we can then recall the Middle English *trouthe, truthe, trewthe, treowthe,* and Anglo-Saxon *trēowþ, trīewþ.* To these words, we associate the Modern English *veracity, faith, fidelity, loyalty, honor, pledge,* and *covenant.* No doubt, the phenomenal experience, disclosed through description, and "proven" in its *being worldly projective,* grounds the possibility for that which has been lost in an economy of *imperium's* domination—namely, *loyalty, honor,* and *pledge.* On a more intimate note, this understanding of the nature of truth as *disclosive of the world* liberates us from the demands of the epistemic tradition, which forces everything into quantification and totality. Plus, what we gain in taking up truth as that which discloses the phenomenal experience is a qualification of the "objective" and a redemption of the "subjective"—whether that be love, hope, or grief. After all, it is only a logical-mathematical requirement that forces hate to be the opposite of love, or happiness to be the opposite of sadness. Anyone who takes an honest look at the dispositions which are signaled in these descriptions will find that neither is one a negation or refinement of the other. Happiness is just as little a negation of sadness as love is a negation of hate. Such dispositions resist such logical-mathematical categorization.

With this definition of truth now firmly established, we may proceed. What remains in the last several chapters of this work is an interrogation into the conditions for the "location" (as the locus of authenticity) such that we can then proceed with the blueprints for constructing the economic infrastructure needed to support truth and authenticity in the emergent project. To do so, we will now supplant the phenomenological method of inquiry by joining it up with reports on empirical investigations—reports which borrow heavily from the psychology of the already mentioned Diana Fosha, by way of the generalist intellectual Bonnitta Roy. An interrogation into individual and group psychology will help draw out the problem of the "I, myself" and explicitly identify the novel subject and novel type of subjectivity which we must animate in the emergent project, if we are to nurture truth and authenticity. Only once we have made this identification can we then return to our inherited infrastructure; only then will we be prepared for real economic reform prescriptions.

Αληθευειν, Foundation for a New Economy

From the outset, the nature of this work has been clear. Prescriptions for nurturing truth and authenticity must fall within the realm of economic reform. After all, it must be admitted, nurturing honesty in any particular *you* or *me* would certainly be disadvantageous for anyone whose environment did not mutually support such disclosure. Therefore, for this work to have value whatsoever, it must reach beyond mere self-help psychology and deliver something resembling prescriptions for economic reform. Of course, in announcing such reform, we should not be too shy to face any hesitations which may arise. Therefore, we should already proceed with one concern that could threaten our confidence in this entire project. After all, we must admit that there is such a thing as *too much honesty*—especially if that disclosure oversteps any personal boundaries, thereby breaking social conventions. In such cases, full disclosure is, quite frankly, *creepy*. And so, what if, in the course of activating our prescriptions, we end up butt naked and, instead of feeling shame, we discover those among us who are grotesquely proud? Even the most fundamental of lived experiences, such as grief, require highly nuanced conditions,

111

such that disclosure is well received. Therefore, in pursuing a path which leads us towards *more disclosure*, we should remember that such conditions do exist in which concealment is appropriate. Inasmuch, any advocates for the authenticity prescribed in this work should not be mistaken as promoting destruction of the sacred or the taboo. Notice how we have been careful not to describe the nature of our reform as a *social* one. Our prescriptions here only seek to nurture the safety and security which truth demands. And in doing so, we leave culture to evolve and police itself.

Now, given this first paragraph, it should be clear that we are entering sensitive territory. No doubt, the realm of human psychology can be discomforting, and we may feel a bit queasy to look for advice within this discipline—certainly when our task is one of economic reform. Plus, we may be too quick to outright reject our venture if we consider the "funny business" of group psychology. Yet at the same time, we should also expect that those researchers who have studied the disciplines of behavioral and group psychology to have also learned a great deal about authenticity. After all, it is here that we find the empirical investigations into a psychology of truth. Therefore, we shall proceed down this particular avenue of research, and we do so vigilant to the dangers which lay in demystifying and capturing the creative spirit into a prison of definitive language. We will use this research to draw out our novel subject and also the primordial *actio*, *αληθευειν* ("to adhere to the unconcealed disclosive in the saying that lets appear")—in turn, this *actio* will then guide our prescriptions for economic reform in the emergent project.

In an unpublished report, *Open to Participate*, the already mentioned generalist intellectual Bonnitta Roy reports on her experience from a business venture taking up exactly this *"psychology of truth"*. Of particular interest are the descriptions which follow from the observation of individuals under the demands of group dynamics—those demands of servicing interpersonal needs and social expectations— dynamics which pose an obstacle to inward reflection. We proceed further with this report, even if in the end we wish to reach something of an organic and ecstatic authenticity beyond sterile facilitator-driven environments. We venture into psychology for transitional and educational language only.

In this document, Roy introduces Collective Participatory Process for Emerging Insight—a facilitated process where the goal is sustaining *coherence* in order to catalyze authentic disclosure. Coherence is defined as *"sustaining participation in the process of making distinctions and revealing difference"*. *"Coherence depends on the full participation of individuals as unique agents in exploring the 'fault lines' where differences verge."* Note that the term *"fault lines"* has been placed in quotation marks. This is significant. In continuing, we find of some importance the description of a definitive state of coherence in which, *"Novel insights emerge from the adaptive processes of diversity-in-co-creative interplay"*. *"Diversity is maintained through high-state coherence"* which *"sets the level that the insight attains"*. Roy's research is founded upon that of the already mentioned psychologist Diana Fosha. In *The Transformative Power of Affect*, Fosha describes this high-state coherence as a state,

> "wherein individuals are deeply in touch with essential aspects of their own experience. Experience is intense, deeply felt, unequivocal, and declarative; sensation is heightened, imagery is vivid, focus and concentration are effortless. Self-attunement and other-receptivity easily coexist. Mindfulness—the

> capacity to take one self, one's world, and one's own
> unfolding experience as objects of awareness and re-
> flection—prevails. The affective marker for core state
> is the truth sense. The truth sense is a vitality affect
> whose felt-sense is an aesthetic experience of right-
> ness...There is an internal experience of coherence,
> cohesion, completion, and essence."

Within the writing of these researchers, we find this state of
coherence referred to as *State four, Core State and the Truth
Sense*. Roy prefaces this by three others: namely, a *"**Conditioning** that creates needs-based interactions, **Deconstruction**
that reveals and releases them, and **Individuation** that leads
to participation and the possibility of cognitive flow"*. Now, let
us not be mistaken, this emphasis on *"fault lines"*, *"individuation"*, and *"sustaining and revealing difference"* does not
suggest that these researchers are interested in merely *tal-
lying the differences*—meaning, counting and accounting for
displays of grievance. And while displays of sympathy and
understanding may preclude coherence, this state is indicated by *novel value creation*, as prior "baggage" is left behind.
This priority on *difference* and *novel value creation*, as characteristics definitive for coherence, should already suggest
the relevance of this research project to our own; it reflects
our hesitation towards the often-sought epistemic narrative
which tells the story of a oneness—of a "humanity", as announced in chapter six of this opuscule. And given all the
terminology that was introduced in the previous chapters,
this four-stage description of the empirical evidence resonates appropriately. In fact, the language used to describe
these states, such as *"conditioning"* and *"individuation"*, is
consistent with that which we have inherited through phenomenological metaphysics. Inasmuch, we can say that this
clinical research confirms that which has been intuitively

felt throughout the testimony of our historical continuum. However, despite this felt practicality of the research, there is unquestionable originality in the report. What we find valuable is the creative spirit at work in Roy's own author-ship—particularly in the description of observed *"creative flow"*. In the document Roy remarks that,

> "Artists and geniuses across the ages have reported this feature of creative flow—where insight and in-spiration seem *to come to one's self from some other place*, but what is required of the person is to build the capacity to *receive* and *presence* it, in feeling, speech and action."

If we look carefully at the words used to express this senti-ment, we find particular interest in *"receive and presence"*, especially in the mediums of *"feeling, speech, and action"*. But in thinking upon these three mediums, a question pres-ents itself, *what could it mean to presence insight from out-side the self in action over-and-above what was already pres-enced in speech?* Of course, this question comes forward in assuming that speech is not exhausted by verbal phenome-na, but also includes in it body language and other observ-able speech behaviors. Therefore, we might also think our question is a bit pedantic. After all, perhaps Roy has simply taken some artistic liberty, adding multiple words where simply *speech* might have sufficed. On this point, we should not be too dismissive. There is a depth worth elucidating—one which we can be certain Roy was aware of herself.

First, we should acknowledge that it would be narrow-mind-ed to think of action as merely some physical-mechanical motion. And in looking beyond the discipline of physics, we find that there is such a thing as motionless action—an action which presences when objects are completely at rest.

This action is present in the object's simply *being there*. It is often successfully explored in science fiction; thus, we can bring to mind H.P. Lovecraft's extraterrestrial in *The Colour from Outer Space*, or Arthur C. Clarke's monolith of *2001: A Space Odyssey* fame. The mere presence of the alien object displaces that which surrounds it simply in its being there. Now, in order to name exactly this action which presences in the object's mere being there, we can return to the language from the first half of this opuscule. In doing so, we remember that αληθευειν is an adherence. Adherence itself is a motionless "action"—a constant action. Adherence is not some motion directed towards things outside of itself, but instead, it is a constant action towards itself as ομοιωσις. If we consider those objects which we normally describe as beautiful, admirable, epic, exotic, or uncanny, we are captivated—captured—in a striking way, such that adherence provokes not merely our action (even explicit cognitive thinking), but a primordial *actio* as reckoning. Only on account of this reckoning can any subsequent mechanical action occur. We could say that only by way of the adherence of the imperial ideal could *verum* come to be, whatsoever. All surveillance and subterfuge throughout the Roman empire were mere mechanical actions in accordance with such an adherence of the imperial ideal. We should not be mistaken; action will always and forever lag behind and chase after the motionless action of adherence.

Of course, truth, as we have inherited it, belongs to the domain of judgement. And it is here, in thinking on *personal judgement*, that we can interpret Roy's tripartite receiving and presencing of insight in *"feeling, speech, and action"*. We might say that adherence to one's personal judgement conditions the breadth of possibilities of an individual's actions. In this case, adherence is something of a social promise by way of one's adherence to their character. The presencing of character, then, conditions the expectations of the moment—including the behavior of everyone who is present. That is to say, the presencing of personal judgement unfolds a social topography. Roy's tripartite, therefore, does not refer us merely towards an internal *feeling* and an external *speech*, but also to the social λογος by which the phenomena of experience come into accord with one another. Here, we are using λογος according to our interpretation of Heraclitus' fragment from the fourth chapter of this opuscule: that by which phenomena come into accord with one another. Amending that interpretation with language from Aristotle, we would then say that λογος is that which sheds light on the whole (καθολου) such that the particulars (καθ εκαστον) relate to that whole in an accordance. That *"accordance"* is *a picture of the world* which constantly proves itself again and again through the adherence as constant action to that accord. And this presencing of one's personal character completes the presencing of insight in *"feeling, speech, and action"*, which we call *authenticity*.

Now, while reference to the Ancient Greek αληθευειν may feel pretentious, we may want to simply translate it as "sincerity", "honesty", or "genuineness". *Αληθευειν* in Modern Greek would be translated as "to truth"—as in, for example, "to walk". However, this interpretation of the Ancient Greek carries with it the epistemological foundationalism of the subject/object relationship on which even the science of psychology is built. Yet, in order to understand the conclusion which Roy draws in her research, it will be helpful to transport our way of thinking out of epistemology's individual-subject. No doubt, Roy's research is founded on Fosha's *"mindfulness"*—a Western appropriation of Buddhist practice. Grounded in *anatta*, this practice draws out the presumption of the individual-subject as "I, myself". Yet, the experience of *anatta* offers only the platitude, "I am not my feelings". And what we discover in releasing ourselves from the ownership of even our own feelings is that there is no subject, no object whatsoever, laying behind the fleeting phenomena of experience. It is in thinking on the constitution of this individual-subject (as that which lies behind the fleeting phenomena of experience) which will allow for an understanding of the economic prescriptions which follow from Roy's research. Therefore, for the sake of digesting those conclusions, we will continue to draw on the phenomenological method of inquiry of Martin Heidegger's lecture course material. It is here that we find language helpful for maintaining our phenomenological commitment. Such language will also allow us to wrest αληθευειν away from any modern translation as *sincerity, honesty,* or *genuineness*.

The question of the individual-subject—that "I, myself "—is a question that, perhaps quite unexpectedly, can be traced back to the priority of human animals over "lesser" animals—a priority which began with the Ancient Greek interpretation of the human condition. The Ancient Greeks believed that before the world was wholly in being, it was merely the realm of natural needs. All animals, for example, orient themselves through αισθησις (*aesthēsis*, "sensual perception"). They seem to have a kind of φρονησις (*fronēsis*, "practical wisdom"). The Ancient Greeks also recognized that animal life makes φωνη (*fonē*, "sound") that coordinates action,

> "As vocalization, speaking is not mere noise, ψοφος (*psofos*), but is ψοφος σημαντικος (*psofos semantikos*), a noise that signifies something; it is φωση and ερμηνεια (*hermēneia*, 'interpretation'): The φωνη is a noise that pertains essential to a living being. Only

animals can produce sounds. The ψυχη (*psūkhe*, 'soul') is the ουσια ζωης (*ousia zois*, 'being alive'), it constitutes the proper being of something that is alive."

Yet, while non-human animals coordinate actions, they do not possess *the whole*. Λογος sheds light on the whole such that the particulars relate to that whole. This is what Heidegger means when he says that human beings and the world are, but they are not quite *there*. Through the luminescence of λογος, they are *da sein* ("being there"). Speaking as uncovering or revealing (αληθεια), according to Heidegger, always means (for Aristotle) speaking and revealing the world to other human beings. Therefore, man's unique being is determined by λογος. For Aristotle, λογος is *the word* in a proper sense—it is language. Therefore, there is a relationship between hearing and the appearance of the world. For Heidegger, this is related to memory and teaching,

> "Hearing, along with speaking, pertains to man's very possibility. Because man can hear, he can learn. Both senses, hearing and seeing, have, in different ways, a privilege: hearing makes possible communication, understanding others; seeing has the privilege of being the primary disclosure of the world, so that what has been seen can be spoken of and appropriated more completely in λογος."

Hearing is, therefore, essential to what we would understand as cultivation, the cultivated, or simply *culture* today. However, we should not burden the Ancient Greeks or Heidegger with such objects—it is, after all, important for our understanding that we do not. Such terminology pertains to sciences such as anthropology and sociology. For us, we turn backward to the ancients, which, perhaps on account of a kind of primitiveness, offers some insight into the essential and phenomenal experience. In Aristotle, we find not *culture* or *society*, but instead the *being* of those having λογος (as *the word, language*) as *a being with one another,* κοινωνια (*koinonia*, "joint participation, a share which anyone has in anything, fellowship, or communion"). The preservation of our humanity (as the *there* of *being*) depends on our capacity for what Aristotle calls αληθευειν (as *revealing* or *uncovering*) in the economy of the πολις (*polis*, "one's city or country"),

> "Insofar as disclosure has for the Greeks the goal of αληθεια, the Greeks designate [disclosure] as αληθευειν, that is, designate it in terms of what is achieved in it, αληθεια. We do not intent to translate this word, αληθευειν. It means to be disclosing, to remove the world from concealedness and coveredness. And that is a mode of being of human *da sein*."

The above three quotations have been reproduced here by way of André Schuwer and Richard Rojcewicz's reconstruction of Heidegger's lecture course material, conducted during the winter semester of 1924-1925 at the University of Marburg. Twenty years later, Heidegger found the confidence to properly define αληθευειν. We repeat his definition once again, as it appears in the lecture course material on Parmenides: *"to adhere to the unconcealed disclosive in the saying that lets appear"*. Heidegger's *"adherence"* to the *"unconcealed"* in the *"saying"* preserves a bias towards that which is produced by the human mouth and by the human hand. *"Adherence"* is action towards the *"saying"*, that is, towards *the word, language*, and the unique being of *"man"*—that which is λογος. Inasmuch, what we find in Heidegger is a pronouncement of the bias which has burdened the Western tradition from the Ancient Greeks through to the works and legacies of Boethius, Avicenna, and Saint Anselm of Canterbury, among others. And while we should not defend Heidegger for continuing with this unfortunate bias, we can understand the value of his work in that it provides for a confrontation with that bias. This housing of λογος in the economy of the πολις is, no doubt, a principal displacement in Western history. Throughout the modernization project, many definitive edges have been given to the πολις. In its widest sense, πολις defines the economy of mankind, the human animal, "humanity"—we can find this use in talks of a "unipolar world", for example. This definition demands itself the delineation of *my* experience as tantamount to *yours*, such that the designation *human* has meaning. Hence the usefulness of concepts like *subjectivity* to describe the condition of that experience. Intersubjectivity, then, extends that condition to others. From here we find ourselves with the problem of intersubjective transcendence. Only by way of this bias can we understand Heidegger's proposed solution to intersubjectivity, the transcendental *mitdasein*. This housing of λογος in the economy of the πολις also leads to the objective position of the sciences—that omniscient world observer which is pronounced in anthropology and sociology, among other disciplines. And it is only in this light that we can understand how countless students, following the lead of professor Hubert Dreyfus, have contemplated the question of whether or not animals or machines could have *da sein* as their way of being." This question is only possible within the Ancient Greek priority of the πολις as the economical domain of λογος. It is today a question which can only be raised as an epistemological question—that is, from a want of extending the being of "man" to nature.

However, if we forgo the subjectification of the "event" of
ομοιωσις—that subjectification which explicitly sets a metaphysical subject "man" apart from the rest of nature, then we
can be delivered from sociological concerns over to a purely phenomenological position. In returning ομοιωσις to the
objective domain—that of nature itself—we then find that
λογος manifests in the phenomena of the heard word or vi-
sual body movements and behaviors, or it comes from phenomena altogether besides those concerning the human animal. Inasmuch, we cannot bring ourselves today to reserve
αληθευειν for a description of a mere human comportment
towards the phenomena of experience. Unlike those ways
of being as described by Aristotle, namely σοφος (*sofos*),
τεχνιτης (*technitis*), or φρονιμος (*fronimos*), αληθευειν (as
that "to truth" which is presenced in λογος) is the comportment of the world wholly. Αληθευειν is the adherence as a
constant action of the world towards itself. It is one which
any individuated "I, myself" is completely subjected to.
From this position we could never ask that we re-supplant
the being of "man" back into nature. Of course, the objection
may be that nature cannot *speak* the truth. But then again,
there is the expression, "I did not believe my own eyes". And
in that case, nature has shown itself; shown itself as what it
is, and that picture was *unbelievable*—that is to say, λογος
had presented the phenomena such that the picture of the
world adhered as *false*. With this final qualification, we now
find ourselves at an appropriate place in our development to
finally define the subject of our opuscule. Just know that we
have not yet finished with αληθευειν. We will use this qualification of αληθευειν in the next chapter, as we link the primordial *actio* of adherence together with mechanical action.

So, what then becomes of our "subject" when the human
animal, "lesser" animals, and machine, finally collapse into

each other? What happens once we have flattened the ontological hierarchy? Already, since the very first chapters of this opuscule, we have acknowledged our primordial condition—that *wheeling and dealing with nature.* As a condition for the description of the objects of the world, *discourse* is prior to all theorizing on any particular appearance of the world. Only on account of this rhythmic harmony with nature is any articulation of objects possible, including any particular *you* or *me.* Any act of speech (whether bodily, verbal, or written) is merely a refinement—a more articulate form of discourse. We remind ourselves that the evidence for such discourse is the very appearance of the world itself. Without it, no common activity could be made to effectively contend with the world, such that the world could be articulated as the world that it is. Therefore, in the event of such a collapse of the special priority of the human animal—heretofore, christened with metaphysical category "man" (a subject over-and-above as uniquely distinct from nature) onto animal and machine, what would then remain is that primordial harmony with nature—that *wheeling and dealing* which alone constitutes a metaphysical subject. We understand discourse as the foundation for even the subject of Descartes's *prima philosophia.* This discourse points towards *"the center"* (Schumacher) as the foundation of *"consciousness,* intellectus archetypus, *or transcendental ego"* (Gadamer), or whatever other name we give to that object to which every worldly object can be traced back. Inasmuch, we must admit that the critique of mindfulness which we considered earlier in this chapter—that which suggests there is no subject, no object whatsoever, laying behind the fleeting phenomena of experience—does not so much ruin the efforts of our psychological researchers, Fosha and Roy; instead, this recognition points us forward, beyond the epistemologist's *tabula rasa*—John Locke's *"white paper"*—that contentless individual-subject which we can now see was prepared for by Plato and, above all, by Aristotle. And while we can say that the Western appropriation of Eastern mindfulness practices manifested by way of the symptoms of industrialized life, we can also admit that this was a form of coping as a kind of preparation.

It is here that we find sense in the conclusions to Roy's research. If we genuinely wish to nurture conditions for truth and authenticity, then we are required to "subjectify" this *dealing. Subject* is a word which comes to us by way of Latin *subiectum, subicio* (from *sub,* "under, beneath, at the foot of" and *iacio,* "I lay, set, establish, build, found, construct"). The present infinitive of *iacio* is *iacere. Fundamenta iacere* means "to lay the foundations". Our subject is, therefore, the subject in a twofold manner. Our subject is both metaphysical, as the condition of possibility, and it is also the subject of our economic reform. This is how we can claim that our economics are *primordial*—a *prima economics* which parallels *prima philosophia.* What we must acknowledge then is that, as a foundation, our subject is not the subject of any mechanical science—one which treats of cause-and-effect—but is instead the foundation on which any *science of economy* can be made possible. Even if only implicitly, this subject was the foundation for the great economic descriptions and their respective pioneers from the past century: John Maynard Keynes, Ludwig von Mises, or Milton Friedman.

Finally, and in line with our interpretations, what we find in the concluding sections of Roy's *Open to Participate* are prescriptions for a reunion with that primordial harmony with nature—through what she calls *"civic engagement"*—as the applicable domain for psychology's State Four, Core State and the Truth Sense,

> "In the past, civic engagement has primarily lever-
> aged human *needs* for connection, sharing and be-
> longing. Yet needs-based action tends to be re-ac-
> tive, not pro-active, functional, not creative, and is
> inadequate to the 21st century imagination fostering
> trans-human and post-human values and realist
> utopian ideals such as eudaemonia, thrivability and
> flourishing. Therefore, going forward, we must rein-
> vent civic engagement as full participation in emer-
> gent *capacities*, such as insight and co-realization."

Yet to do this, we require not some self-focused training or
"an art of attunement", but rather an economic practice,

> "We must move beyond merely *modelling* complex
> adaptive systems, to *in vivo* simulations of them,
> to actual immersion in participatory processes that
> enact them. And since complex adaptive systems,
> by definition, are non-linear and not reproducible,
> we will not be able to derive such practices through
> rules and fixed methodologies, but through meta-de-
> sign principles for creating, and 'model-free' process
> methodologies for facilitating practices that can cata-
> lyze emergent capacities."

Roy's words should not be read too quickly. Consider an
economy in which *"thrivability"* is paramount to *"sharing"*,
and *"flourishing"* is paramount to *"belonging"*. And yet, at
the same time, imagine this economy beyond any motivations which could be described through the psychological
toolkit, including diagnoses such as greed or selfishness.
There is depth worth elucidating here. It is clear that for
Roy, the presencing of insight (what we have called *authenticity*, that which manifests through feeling, speech, and
αληθευειν) is conditioned by civic engagement. However,

it is not entirely apparent why authenticity must manifest through such engagement, or why another form of social value-adding engagement could not suffice. What constitutes civic engagement? Why is it classed as engagement at all? And why must that engagement be civic? Only in answering these questions can we come to understand the type of economic reform which could nurture encounters with the truth. Therefore, we take these questions seriously. First, to answer the question of *engagement*, we must expand our metaphysical architectonic. We must come to understand the "venue" for truth. Likewise, to answer the question of *the civic* we must understand the "forum" in which truth is conditioned.

The Encounter as the Venue for Truth

In thinking on the historical economy of truth presented in the first half of this opuscule, there can be no hiding the pejorative character which was given to doubt. However, our narrative would be ignorant if it were to dismiss doubt altogether. After all, *doubt* is a word which has been used to help describe a whole collection of real phenomena—phenomena to which each of us can likely attest to. If we consider that *experience*, that is, the *real* phenomenological experience of doubt, then we should, of course, expect many varying descriptions. However, we can also assume a few common characterizations. An attentive focus, for example—one which is motivated by a desire for relief to mental discomfort. We might say that this discomfort demands for the presence of λογος, such that the phenomena of our experience come into accord with one another—such that a logical consistency presents the world over to us as a whole. Inasmuch, doubt offers an explicit example of an *ecstasy of time*—a moment which arises from out of the habitual experience of the day-to-day—such that we meet *the world as an intellectual encounter*. This encounter with the world is the very "venue" in which a disclosure of the truth is possible.

Now, while doubt proves itself to be a good condition (or one possible ingredient) for the disclosure of truth, we must also admit that it is merely just one such condition/ingredient. And, it does not exhaust the possibilities for the disclosure of truth. Consider, even, the rather trivial task of entering a room, for example. After all, while there may be countless operations which are performed without even thinking about it (and if we are to break down the process of entering a room thusly: operating the door latch, operating the door hinges, even bodily walking), there is also the possibility that in executing this task, you discover that the door is, in fact, stuck in a closed position. And, in this case, we might expect that your world conforms to a physical or mechanistic $\lambda o\gamma o\varsigma$, as resolving the obstruction then becomes the task itself. However, we would be fooling ourselves if we were to believe that physics and a physical description of the world exhausted all the possibilities presented at the encounter. If, for example, the door is in a public space, then a variety of social obstructions might appear before you in your mind's eye. It could be that someone has intentionally locked the door, for example. Perhaps there is an event happening inside the room which should not be disturbed. The point is that an encounter with the world not only opens up a space for the disclosure of the logical-mathematical, but a robust world—whether the articulation of the world has been conditioned by the epistemologist's predisposition to doubt, or by the simple task of passing into a room in a public building. And while we would describe the world as singular—as "one's world"—that world is full of a variety of objects. From food and chairs, to feminism and liberty.

Now, it may seem as if some of the language which we have taken up in this opuscule is in contradiction. For example, when we talk of *"the world as a whole"* and at the same time criticize any description of a "uni-verse" (as an object promising a totality). Yet, this contradiction is only apparently so. Insofar as the objects presenced at the encounter may or may not conform to mathematical quantification, these objects resist ordering into a schematic such that a singular totality could ever be made. Contrary to such totalization, we may even find that once having drawn our definitions, we then discover one or more phenomena that may be multi-stable. For instance, Rubin's vase becomes two opposing faces with a change of focus. Inasmuch, we must admit that any one description of phenomena could never be more or less universally appropriate than another. Lightning, for example, is not tantamount to or merely a type of electromagnetic discharge. At most, we could say that the description *electromagnetic discharge* is a refinement of the description *lightning*. To think otherwise would be to put the cart before the horse, as the expression goes. The articulation of any object is only possible from out of that pre-intellectual, or pre-cognitive, primordial discourse—that *wheeling and dealing with nature*. Any object which captures and defines a phenomenal experience is always and forever appropriate in the commerce to which it belongs. Indeed, it is the appropriateness which stabilizes the phenomena, such that its adherence is experienced.

Given the polylogical possibilities inherent in the nature of each encounter, we can surmise a certain qualification to our project at hand. If we are to genuinely nurture truth and authenticity, then we must overcome the monological bias which we have inherited. From the Roman Empire to the Catholic Inquisition and the industrialized sciences, the language of Latin has carried with it the monotheistic residue of imperial economy—that economy which seeks a quantified and totaled "uni-verse". And yet, it really should be no surprise that the romanticized picture of the polytheistic agricultural civilizations calls for our attention. While we could never forgo the expediency which industrial manufacturing has provided to the production of food, housing, transportation, and other goods and services, it is still all-too enjoyable to picture ourselves out of this technological luxury. We imagine every action, from the tiling of the land to the collection of the harvest, as a communication, or κοινωνια (koinonia, "communion"), with our most supreme idols. For the ancients, labor flattered their idols. Those idols adhered through such flattery, and that flattery was requited back through the bounty of the labor. Of course, what should not be dismissed as primitive is the plurality of those gods. After all, primitiveness is exactly its own positive characteristic. Primitive points towards the primordial. Plurality itself echoes the multi-stable character of the encounter—a characteristic of the encounter which was jeopardized already in a Christianization of Rome. It is not a coincidence that in overcoming "man" as a metaphysical category and in animating *the human animal as something natural*, we also animate our pagan heritage.

Now, this turn towards labor as an example in this exposition is not accidental. Labor, as the political expression of the primordial *wheeling and dealing with nature*, points us towards value creation outright. That is to say, laboring produces the objects which we know as values *towards living*—not merely the aforementioned food and chairs, or feminism and liberty, but also truth. This is to say, discourse produces the objects of our world in the most robust sense. And, while it may feel inhumane to say, this includes even the "production" of any objectivized *you* or *me*. Returning once again to *Small is Beautiful*, we recall that E.F. Schumacher writes of a harmony with nature as a work which *"brings forth a **becoming existence**"*. Existence *becomes—* that is, existence is presenced and intellectually refreshed in each moment of articulation. In this moment of articulation, the mechanical and social topography of the world is announced. Equally, a history is announced. History unfolds through the succession of mechanical objects which we know as belonging to time, and through such presencing, we find ourselves animated—pulled towards—that causal chain of events. Such a feedback loop with nature has been characterized psychologically as a *"cognitive flow"* (Mihaly Csikszentmihalyi)—a process of challenge and resolve. It is with this understanding that we proceed with labor as the political expression of the conditions necessary for the encounter as the venue for truth.

Insofar as this is the case, any prescriptions for nurturing truth requires that we address the conditions for this encounter. And because the encounter is possible anytime and anywhere, we cannot fool ourselves into thinking that nurturing truth simply demands venues for truth—scheduled meetings with "safe rules", say. Prescriptions for nurturing truth would be unbelievably naïve if they simply suggested juried townhalls for deliberation such that, at the end, everyone walked away having possession of the truth. No. Nurturing truth demands that we respect the natural environment in which we find it—that *wheeling and dealing* which manifests through the labor of the project and can be recalled at the most trivial of places—the airport, the coffee shop, or a neighbor's patio barbecue party.

Of course, there is a contrary understanding, popularly held by the progenitors of industrialization—one which is accepted by both employer and employee—that labor is ultimately something which is to be reduced and preferably obliterated. "Labor is expensive", says the employer. And for the employee, labor takes time away from pleasure. He is made to believe that he is something of a hedonist—that the natural condition of human existence is pure sensual satisfaction. The hourly worker is paid for his time from such pleasure. Such understanding gives cause for a prophecy—that one day, an automatized manufacturing system will relieve the human animal from his fetters. This day will constitute some kind of *holy day* for the human animal, and then we can all go on *holiday*. And yet, standing here in this very moment, in this *"time between worlds"*, we understand the folly of this understanding. An automatization of labor could mean nothing other than the death of truth. Alternatively, a reunion of that which was separated early in industrial-liberation's church and state—or rather, *belief and action*—promises a reunion with the primordial harmony with nature. This redemption promises a re-communion with nature, such that nature may once again bless us with its bounty.

Having now come to understand the encounter as the venue for truth, a moment which is conditioned by a primordial *wheeling and dealing*—that which we understand through its political expression as labor—we are prepared to answer the first of our questions posed at the end of the previous chapter. We are prepared to answer any challengers as to why it must be exactly *engagement* that constitutes our prescriptions for nurturing truth and authenticity. Yet, what remains is the second of our questions—an understanding of *the civic* as a type of labor. Does civic engagement simply mean volunteering in food drives or taking lonely elderly for walks? Of course, it may feel overly obvious that civic engagement of this type might solve our sense of alienation, rootlessness, estrangement, and apathy which we have announced as our principal motivation for our investigations. Yet, it is not entirely apparent just exactly how civic engagement will nurture the alternative to episteme, outright—that alternative which we have identified as $\alpha\lambda\eta\theta\varepsilon\nu\varepsilon\iota\nu$. Therefore, in the following chapter, we will quest in search of those connections.

Δημιουργος and the Proximity of Αληθευειν

We have arrived at the tenth chapter of this opuscule, and we are now a long way from the inception. Despite this, we carry forward our original provocation—a dissatisfactory commitment to truth from within our inherited economy. Our dissatisfaction is underlined by a sense of alienation, rootlessness, estrangement, and apathy—symptoms which have given rise for the want of truth and authenticity. In the previous chapter, we qualified *the encounter* as the "venue" for truth. This encounter is a moment conditioned by a pre-intellectual, or pre-cognitive, *wheeling and dealing with nature*—that which we understand through its political expression as *labor*. This laboring provides for the "event" of authenticity. And within this event, the phenomenal experience is brought into accord, such that the world announces itself as the world which it is. The adherence of the world then calls after our action. Through adherence, we can speak the truth of the world and the world can be put into motion. Inasmuch, we are now prepared to answer any challengers as to why *engagement* must ground our prescriptions for nurturing truth and authenticity. Yet, what remains is the second of our questions—why must that engagement be *civic?* And in continuing the project to establish our metaphysical architectonic, we must ask, *what constitutes the civic as a type of labor?*—one which, for example, could be compared or contrasted to others.

Firstly, then, let us begin with *civic* as a mere word. Looking at our historical texts, we can trace *civic* back to Latin. Here, we find the word *civicus* ("pertaining to a city, or citizens"). Within *civicus*, we find the noun *civitas* ("city"). We can further trace this word back to the root noun *civis* ("citizen"). Perhaps, quite uninterestingly, we can say that the civic pertains to the commerce of the citizenry. Yet, at the same time, we should not be too dismissive. What should not be overlooked is that this framing of the citizen is only possible from the exterior—that is, from the position of the one who measures and determines *the citizen* as such. This *who* is *the ruler* by which the citizen is to be measured—the king, the consul, or the emperor. The subject for this king is the one who lies below him, as *subiectum*, and is to be measured up against him as a standard. And while it may feel as though this relationship (namely, that between the king and his subject, the citizenry) is archaic, this is not the case—there is depth worth elucidating here.

Recalling the second chapter of this opuscule, we can remember our initial talk of rulers by way of positivism; more specifically, we can remember our talk of objective standardization. We can also remember that the project to describe the phenomenal experience of nature had proven objective standardization as an invaluable tool for the measurement of the physical world. However, what cannot be ignored is the application of objective standardization within the realm of later scientific pursuits. In recalling the sixth chapter of this opuscule, we can remember the application of such standardization within the science of sociology. Within this discipline, the individual (whether an objectivized *you* or *me*) is measured up against the subject matter, *society*. In that chapter, the epistemological sociologists, and the Scandinavian metamodernists in particular, served as our example. Of course, this ruler, society, is quite well concealed in intellectual pursuits such as the ones in which these sociologists are involved—the ruler wears a mask of intellectual guise, so to speak. However, this method of "ruling", as a successor to the relationship between the king and his subject, the citizenry, becomes strikingly evident in the brute force of political activism. Let us continue our elucidation on this type of ruling by using the Body Positive Movement as our example. Within this political movement, we find that society serves as the location for a transposition of private judgement—that is, the characteristically "interior" private judgement is transposed onto the "exterior" society. Speaking psychologically, we say that *society is the object on which the private aesthetic valuation has been projected.* In the mouth of the Body Positive movement activist, then, it is not I who holds the beauty standard which offends me (because that would seem paradoxical to the activist), but instead, it is society who holds that standard. This new location of aesthetic judgement is, then, not only that which houses the standard for judgement; it is also both a substantial object and a new ruler by which we measure beauty (as opposed to the object, *me*, as the individual-subject). Hence, we speak of the reification of society. The ambition of the Body Positive activist, then, is to expand the measuring rod by which his or her own-most (personal) society understands the beautiful, such that more can be included.

Now, it should also be said that we are not particularly interested in ruining the efforts of those activists. Let us be fair—identifying a psychological projection at work within these activists and their actions does not mean that we should dismiss their suffering outright. That would, after all, be quite inhumane. And, after all, we are not here to take sides in any political debate, either. Not to be mistaken, this function of "society" (when in the hands of the sociologist, and as a political tool especially) is not limited to the Body Positive movement, nor to any other form of woke activism. This usage can equally be found within the gang weed Joker meme, *we live in a society*. Of course, this meme takes a different direction by mimicking the profound sentiments demanded by their society. However, as in the case of *we live in a society*, irony accompanies mimicry. "*We live in a society...*" calls our attention to the monologues which follow, "*...where the Kardashians are millionaires and academics can't afford health care*". No doubt, the popularity of this meme attests to the abundance of cynicism found in both the woke and the dissident alike. But, inasmuch, it also attests to its trivialization. *We live in a society* underlines the fact that, today, everyone is something of an "armchair sociologist". Both the woke and the dissident circle within the same $\lambda o\gamma o\varsigma$, or that which measures the authors of such propaganda by the same *ruler*—that of a substantial and reified *society*. Resting this case, we can now move on to the relevance of such psychological projection to our argument at hand. No doubt, psychological projection can help us to understand *the civic* as it pertains to the domain of the social, whether that be within the relationship *king to subject*, or, as today, in the relationship *activist to society*.

Of course, given the pejorative character of *imperium* which was presented throughout the first half of this work, we should be well-prepared enough to take caution when dealing with the civic through these types of social relationships. No doubt, these relationships can only animate the relativity of truth, setting conditions that are ripe for the true and the false of *imperium's* domination and the social power paradigm. However, despite our caution, our investigation into the Latin heritage of *civic* has not been fruitless. After all, the eighth chapter of this opuscule made good use of Ancient Greek vocabulary. This proved useful for drawing out particular distinctions of our Latin heritage. Therefore, we should not be surprised to find an elucidation to our question regarding civic engagement by contrasting Latin and Ancient Greek words. Firstly, then, so as not to be mistaken, let us admit that in Ancient Greece, there too existed a ruler by which the citizen was to be measured. And yet, when looking into the etymology, we find that the citizen is not measured against the king, the consul, or the emperor, and surely not society, but instead to the δημος ("the public, the people"). Yet, in identifying this object, we have not made explicit the ruler by which the πολιτης (*politēs*, "citizen") is to be measured. At first glance, it may look like *civis* can simply be translated into πολιτης. However, when looking into the root word of πολιτης—namely, πολις (*polis*, "one's city or country")—we notice a different root noun from that of *civis* ("citizen"). Let us now explain what that difference might mean.

Today, it is trivial to remember that for the Ancient Greeks, αγαθον (*agathon*, "the good") was paramount. But good for who, or for what, exactly? The ancients lived in an economy of ποιησις (*poiēsis*, "creation, production"), but not merely as a commerce with a material substrate. This was an economy of the presencing of ιδεα; that is, the presencing of the outward appearance of the world within the commerce of the public usage of things and of communal life. We find recorded testaments alluding to this essential experience of ποιησις by way of the writing of the ancients, including

Plato, among others. We can make a case using Plato's *Charmides* as an example. Recalling that dialogue, we remember Socrates' interrogation into the virtue of σωφροσυνη (sō-frosynē, "temperance") together with the Athenian noble Critias. A definition is put forward: *temperance is knowing oneself*. Yet, this definition provokes an objection. Socrates then explains himself,

> "If temperance is a knowing, obviously it must be a kind of science, and it must be a science of something, must it not? | If I were asked if medicine, as a science of health, is useful to us, and what it produces | I should say it is of very great benefit, since it produces health; an excellent result. | And so, if you should ask me what result I take to be produced by building, as the builder's science, I should say houses; and it would be the same with the other arts."

> "Now it is for you, Critias, in your turn, to find an answer to a question regarding temperance—since you say it is a science of self—and to tell me what excellent result it produces for us."

Now, let us ignore the fact that Critias fails to produce an answer which satisfies Socrates throughout this dialogue. And let us never mind the fact that the dialogue itself does not indicate any conclusive definition of temperance. After all, our point *here* has already been made. Producing and production are paramount in the Ancient Greek experience, as evidenced in the writing. So, what then does this mean for us in qualifying the ruler of standard within Ancient Greece? And, more to the point, what does this mean for us in qualifying civic engagement? In Ancient Greece, we do not find language for measuring the citizen as *civis*—that is, through the commerce of the *subiectum*, as the subject in relation to the king, the consul, or the emperor. Instead, we find language for measuring the citizen as δημιουργος *(dēmiurgos, "creator, craftsman")*, compared against the πολις—or rather, the economy of the πολις. Let us not ignore the fact that, for the Ancient Greeks, ποιητικη was not merely the activity of the craftsman, the τεχνιτης; it was equally that of the πολιτικος, the politician. The δημιουργος is that which presences the ιδεα of the δημος through any and all walks of life. Every citizen, as a citizen, has δημιουργος as their way of being. Let us conclude this argument by making our contrast between the Ancient Greeks and the Romans more explicit; for the Greeks, the citizen is measured in terms of production towards his people. In Roman, however, we find a social dialectic in which the subject is measured against another human animal acting as the ruler. This is evidenced in the very objects of the Latin language, as we have made clear.

Yet, even with such a successful contrast between the Ancient Greek and Latin words, haven't we now encountered a difficulty? After all, have we not stated a problematizing of the πολις in previous chapters? And that, in order to recover truth from relativism and return it back to nature, we must encourage a collapse of any definitive boundary of the πολις? In fact, we had. Therefore, in acknowledging the *economy of the city* as a seemingly more favorable ruler by which we measure the citizen in our reformation project at hand, we must now also bring the πολις into a definition which is in accordance with this project. And while we may feel unprepared for this, it is still easily accomplished all the same. What we find within a collapse of any definitive boundary of the πολις—whether as city, nation, or "humanity" in general—is the "radius" of the primordial *wheeling and dealing*. The evidence for this radius can be found everywhere we look. The craftsman's workshop is arranged according to ergonomics. The office worker's keys on the keyboard. Even the automated assembly line, devoid of any human whatsoever, is arranged under the schematic of proximity. Therefore, we must redefine the πολις—which for us, must refer to the "radius" of discourse in nature and together with the natural. The adherence of αληθευειν within this radius pulls us inwards. At the epicenter of the radius, we find the locus of creation, authenticity, at that moment which we have named *the encounter*. The action at this moment produces articulation; it produces definition and, in some cases, description. Therefore, we can say that the πολις is the "forum" of truth. And since discourse is itself grounded upon projection, we can say that projection (or simply, the project) is *the essence of the political. The project* is the center-gravity, which pulls us towards its center-pole. The project, then, as projection, is the ruler by which truth is to be measured against. The relationship under consideration is, then, not between the δημιουργος and the δημος, exclusively, but between the δημιουργος and the πολις, thusly defined. So, when we talk of civic engagement, we are talking of an engagement within the radius which is the πολις. Inasmuch, we understand civic engagement as essentially *pole-itical*. This is why we have referred to labor as *the political expression of the moment of the encounter* throughout the second half of this opuscule. And with this qualification, we have now answered the question posed at the inception of this chapter. We are now better prepared to answer any challengers as to why engagement, as the prescription for nurturing truth and authenticity, must be civic. We have also now, by the way, completed the architectonic of truth which began with the first chapters of the second half of this opuscule.

Now, while we have gone to quite extreme efforts to prove our architectonic of truth in language, history, and by way of appeal to the phenomenal experience, we still owe it to ourselves to continue a procedure which, by now, has become common practice for us—we must, in full sincerity, bring our own conclusions under interrogation. And besides, this is all-too easily done. We should, after all, expect any reader of this opuscule to be well-prepared for such an interrogation. First, we might ask ourselves the question, *are not these appeals to the ancients and to proximity outright conservative*? Certainly, in light of the material benefits produced of a globalized economy, appeals to locale have been seen as anachronistic, isolationist, and (at their worst) manifestations of underlying xenophobia. And there is also a pressing technological objection. Not only has transportation brought the people of different ethnicities and nations within arm's reach, but communication technology too, and specifically those platforms provided of the internet, should prove to us that our proximal *wheeling and dealing with nature* has reached global expanse. By way of these and other planetary technologies, the human body has been augmented with paraphernalia such that we are wont to call our experience *post-human*. According to this narrative, the human animal is now at the hands of the god *technology*, which is, after all, that by which our modern economy functions. This is, no doubt, a clever move by the accelerationists and other proponents of technological solutions to modern problems. However, we should not be seduced into rejecting our appeals to the ancients and to proximity without further clarifying proximity. What should be noted is that proximity, as we are using the word here in this chapter, belongs to our *metaphysical architectonic*. As such, to speak of *proximity* as *locale* is incorrect. The proximal is not tantamount to locale, even if, for the most part, local canvases

143

are where we find a proximal *wheeling and dealing*. And so, while civic engagement may be local and within, say, the city, it may also not be. With remote working a real possibility nowadays, each one of us will have to consider the relationships between both the proximal and the locale more penetratingly in whatever considerations we undertake in reforming the economy. Because, after all, and despite these objections, the proximal *wheeling and dealing* lies beneath, as a foundation for whatever commerce technology may host.

What should be clear, then, as we stand within the *here* and *now* of today in this liminal *"time between worlds"*, is that *first economics* has announced itself because the venue of industrial laboring—the proximal workspace of *wheeling and dealing*, that which we have qualified as the condition for truth—has proven itself unable to support truth. Concisely, we say *the relationship between discourse and truth has become obscured*. This statement strikes us as rather dire; it *should* strike us as dire. We take as our evidence the previously mentioned symptoms of alienation, rootlessness, estrangement, and apathy. And while these psycho-sociological diagnoses may very well be true, we would also do well to consider the consequences of obscuring this relationship to democracy. While we have already qualified democracy as one form of governance which is produced of the national ideal, we should equally qualify democracy as one form of governance in which truth matters to the human animal. And yet, forms of governance of this type are in jeopardy once the relationship between discourse and truth has become obscured. Again, we do not make such a dire claim in order to be dramatic. Quite the contrary, in fact. And we do make this claim in complete sobriety. After all, there can be no doubt as to the real possibility of a furthered domestication of the human animal from within the project of industrial-liberation—a domestication which might be accomplished by way of an algorithmic digitization. Therefore, what is at stake is nothing short of a loss of truth as an object which matters within the commerce of the human animal and, specifically to the point, a loss of truth as an object which matters to the governance of this animal. Of course, we may perhaps find those among us who actually desire such a state of governance—those who would prefer to have no concerns about the truth, as well as to have no say over the truth, either. Even today, we hear from those who would encourage a collapse of democracy down to an algorithmic digitization, and we need not even turn towards the "radical" accelerationists to help make our case. Consider how many people alive today who would insist that only a BlockChain-like technology will be able to solve the age-old problem of corruption. Presumably, this solution would be desirable because we could all then go on busying ourselves with tasks other than disclosing truth. Of course, it seems obvious that any future human animals living underneath this type of governance would experience the meaning of *ουσια ζωης* in a fundamentally different way than we do today. This possibility of future governance is worth considering, even if it falls outside the scope of our development here.

Despite this, and for those of us with more *conservative* tendencies (and this must mean for us only that we wish to conserve truth and those forms of governance in which truth matters), we must now proceed into what we have coined here in this opuscule, namely, *first economics* philosophy. This is the case whether we do so using the language of "*first economics*" explicitly or not. And this is because this realm of thought, and *only* this realm of thought, brings with it a solution. Of course, even if we do take up this philosophy, then we should not simply expect that our future to be well-prepared for, and that solving alienation, rootlessness, estrangement, and apathy is going to be all-too easy. What is required of us, firstly, is an acknowledgement which, to be honest, we have not adequately prepared ourselves for throughout our development. We must acknowledge an enslavement which each one of us, seemingly throughout history and up to this very moment, has been subjected to. This is not an enslavement to capital or to any other worldly slave owner. It is, to be sure, a self-enslavement—whether it be by way of the epistemologist's holy *reason*, the liberal's holy *liberty*, the conservative's holy *tradition*, the modernist's holy *progress*, or the accelerationist's *technology*. Once we acknowledge our enslavement to such holy rulers, then, and only then, can we relieve ourselves of the fetters of the domestication projects to which these rulers belong. Only then can we meet with genuine truth and authenticity here on the surface of the earth. And while it may be easy for any one of us to sacrifice one or more of the previously mentioned *reason, liberty, tradition, progress,* or *technology*, we must equally be willing to forsake that ruler of the Body Positive movement, Black Lives Matter and white nationalism, feminism, and Greta Thunberg-style climate change activism. That is, we must forsake that ruler who looks down to us from above, who requires offerings and sacrifices, who makes dramatic displays of violence when not satisfied by such offerings. We must forsake that god which we know as *society*. We trust that only in forsaking this god can the Body Positive activist, or any other social activist, find satisfactory relief from their master. And only then can epistemology and the domestication project genuinely end. This ruler has been given particular attention throughout our development, since, in our liminal *here* and *now*, it seems to have been given utmost priority by our contemporaries, even usurping physics as the explain-all science of the time. These contemporaries seem to suppose that economics, and especially liberal economic policy, have been historically decided upon and that no further reflections are necessary. This must be a miscalculation on their part.

Of course, having announced an acknowledgement of our own self-enslavement, as a preliminary requisite for nurturing truth and authenticity, we should also make clear the fact that our own subject, *discourse*, is equally one such ruler. After all, the subject of *first economics* philosophy can equally fall within the same category as any of the previous gods which have been worshiped here on the surface of the earth. Discourse is,

Firstly, that which we are subject to,

Secondly, that which produces value through us, and

Thirdly, that by which we measure value.

However, what should already be obvious to anyone by now is the novelty of the domain in which our ruler resides. Discourse occupies a different dwelling; as *subiectum* (or, as that which *establishes, builds, founds,* and *constructs* from *under, beneath,* and *at the foot of*), it is that which lies *below,* as the foundation for the creation of both our highest and lowest values. In the most robust sense, it is that which conditions the production of the objects which we know as *values towards living*—whether we are speaking of liberty, or freedom, or even truth. This includes even the conditioning of the production of every god, whether we are speaking of one within our current time, of the past, or any god which we may meet with in the future. The moment of the encounter, then, is the location between these two spheres. It is *there* where authenticity may manifest as the locus of creation and where the world may present itself afresh, as the world which it is and which it has always been.

Of course, having confronted *first economics* philosophy, a question presents itself. *Are we prepared for such an inversion?* That is, are we prepared for a ruler unlike one which anyone has had before?—not one as a holy virtue or holy ideal—not one which can be worshipped through myth or through any religious practices at all. Are we prepared for a *God from Below*, so to speak? In answering this question, there is also the dire consideration of whether or not we are prepared for a ruler which is utterly unknowable? Let us not forget that we have admitted that discourse is pre-linguistic and pre-cognitive. As such, it resists any appropriation into either language or knowledge. At the closing of the first half of this opuscule, we said that we were moving into a realm which is *a priori*. Perhaps now it is clear: this was not meant as an aggrandizement. Of course, the shadow of this god is indicated in the idolization of *the positive fact* and the essential economy of *parse to transcend*. It is also indicated through the primordial *actio*—whether that be *episteme* or *αληθεύειν*. However, we can only point towards the shadow of our *form of life*, at best. As such, any appeals to our "god" will have a *primordial* character about them.

Now, as precarious as this inversion may seem, examples of certain political activity can be taken as an indication that our futural-historical continuum is moving in this direction. By turning towards those indications in the next couple of chapters, we will present concrete examples which testify to the actuality of our *"god"*. What should be obvious, given what has been elucidated over the course of our development, is that the period of the industrial-liberation project (in which truth was disclosed through public touchpoints, such that the electoral process could direct the course of a nation) resides in the past. This has been indicated by nothing other than the climax of sociology as the explain-all science of the time, and by the social justice activism of the early third millennium. Both this science and this activism indicate that the electoral process, as a barometer of truth, is unsatisfactory. Equally, this indicates to us that if we are to nurture truth in the emergent project, then we cannot simply *ask the people what they want*. And, after all, without appropriate venues for truth, they may not know what would reasonably satisfy their desires. This, of course, is not to say that some government administrators know better on account of access to industry expert information. Certainly, *you* and *me*, sitting here together with this opuscule, do not know either. However, what it does mean is that if we wish to nurture truth in the emergent project—a truth which may project us towards *the good, the beautiful,* and *the just*—then truth itself demands of us appropriately-scaled proximal venues for disclosure. If we understand democracy—that is, a rule by the people—not from the perspective of top-down government administration, but in the sense of communal economy, then truth demands of us suitable mechanisms of *economic democracy* by which it can show itself.

If we continue thinking of democracy as an economic activity, and then apply the aesthetic periodization which was introduced in the closing chapters of the first half of this work, then we are granted a new perspective on exactly those "suitable" mechanisms. Repeating previous chapters, liberal values established *liberal governance* mechanisms. We call these our democratic institutions: electoral processes, freedom of the press, the right to bear arms, *et cetera*. However, those institutions have proven themselves to be satisfactory only insofar as they allow for *social governance* mechanisms. From the perspective of social governance, thinking of governance as merely top-down government administration is not only unsatisfactory, but also archaic. Consider, as an example, the social justice warrior's fight against *the system* itself. Yet, we can say that a similar dissatisfaction belongs to social governance as well. Simply recall the tactics of social *governance as law*: social legislation, surveillance, and punishment. Neither does this represent the entirety of governance. For sure, *governance as law*, whether it be liberal or social, neglects exactly what the church, for example, meant to satisfy in the whole of human economy. Inspiration. Hope. Communion. What should be kept in mind, then, is that in thinking about governance through the lens of economy (in particular, the political activity of the δημιουργος), we are not suggesting to abandon either liberal or social governance mechanisms. Instead, we are suggesting something else altogether—something grounded and built upon liberal and social governance mechanisms. There is reason for why our historical narrative was necessary before the prescriptions. Only *here* and *now*, equipped with our own narrative, can we suggest a governance of *creative production*. Let us keep this in mind as we proceed into our reform prescriptions.

Of course, given our appeals to proximity, we should not be surprised if we were to find mechanisms of said *"economic democracy"* already emerging in those locales where we likewise find the conservative spirit. After all, the spirit for conservation has historically championed locale, as a place of climate and soil, of danger, and of needs and work. Certainly, this is the case following modern transportation and communication technologies. And yet, what should be obvious to anyone living *here* and *now* is that any conservation project—or one which conserves the *status quo*, whether that be industrial-liberation or any other product of liberal values—will likely only further obscure the relationship between discourse and truth. Therefore, we should also not be surprised to find champions for proximal civic engagement reaching across the traditional political spectrum, of both conservative and progressive ends. Margaret Kohn's *Radical Space, Building the House of the People*, perhaps offers one of the best examples. In that work, Kohn appeals to challenge the *"widespread suspicion that a political appeal to place is conservative, essentialist, or anachronistic"*. She explicitly champions for *"a political approach to community that mobilizes the resources of locality"*. Furthermore, and mirroring Bonnitta Roy's prescriptions, Kohn calls for civic engagement and a political approach which *"involves citizens in governing through participation"*, a governance which *"blurs the line between state and civil society"*. She is thoroughly progressive. In the coming chapters, we will turn towards nascent political activity which indicates and highlights mechanisms of economic democracy. And, as this opuscule comes to a close, we will use these as inspiration for describing our own economic reform prescriptions.

Yet, before doing so, we must address the concerns that our subject, our *God from Below* and ruler, is unknowable. In the next chapter, we must reframe the paradigm of our own inquiries into the nature of this god. To do so, we will now turn towards the barometer by which we can gauge the successes or failures of our reform, or any economic reform proposals whatsoever. Perhaps quite unexpectedly, and following all of the polemics of this chapter, we now turn towards an affirmation of the object *society* in the next chapter.

Societas as the Barometer of Truth

At times throughout this opuscule, we have been critical towards the position of *"the omniscient world observer"*—that which we find in, for example, sociology and anthropology. And this has been, on one account, due to the reification of the subject matter of these sciences—namely, the reification which has produced the substantial object, *society*. Now, of course, in saying this, we must also admit to ourselves that we can, after all, understand the position of these scientists, this subject matter, and this object. And we can, of course, understand what society means colloquially, as we find it, for example, within the internet news journals. We understand to which projects this word belongs, and to which actions our attention is to be directed. However, to understand something *"colloquially"* may mean that it is only the activity prescribed by the word which has revealed itself, but that the intellectual object may nevertheless still remain hidden. And, after all, if we are to honour our phenomenological commitment, then we must admit that society is actually a quite difficult phenomenon to *see*. We should not be surprised that the phenomenon to which this word refers has indeed remained hidden. After all, while it is true that we could refer to some mass of material bodies with descriptions such as *the women, the children,* or even *the police*!, we must also admit that it would be very awkward to declare, "there, society!" At best, it seems that, as a substantial object, society manifests as a statistic representing a certain set of dispositions, opinions, and behaviors of a certain set of human animals. Even in the discussions on public health, for example, our object at hand is not the material bodies of the public, but the public as a statistic. Yet, despite this seemingly occult nature of society, we should not assume that the phenomenon captured by that word is irrelevant to our project—only, if we wish to continue to operate with this word, we must appropriately place the phenomenon of society within our architectonic of truth and value creation. This means that we must understand "society" from within *first economics* philosophy. And while these may seem like topics of mere academic interest, and might therefore on that account, appear quite pedantic, it is only in bringing society into our own project that we can understand it as the rightful barometer by which to gauge the success or failure of our reform proposal. Importantly, by way of an explication of this barometer, we will meet the first of many prescriptions by which we might come to honor that unknowable ruler and *God from Below*—discourse.

Now, as is our practice, let us firstly investigate society by way of an etymological study. In doing so, we come to the Latin root words *societas* and *societatum*—these words refer us to Modern English words, such as *fellowship, association, alliance, union,* and *community*. Of course, presented as we are with this collection of words, what becomes strikingly apparent is that society does not owe its origin to references of some material mass, but rather to something social instead. Although, even so, if we were to look for the phenomenon of something like *fellowship* or *union*, then we must still admit that society is still a difficult phenomenon to see. We may want to recall internal feelings, or perhaps more specifically, we may want to recall those feelings of *wholesomeness*, or *being one with the external world as a whole*. Sigmund Freud seems to have referred to this feeling by repeating a patient's description—*"the oceanic feeling"* (*Civilization and Its Discontents*). However, what is important to note is that, even in the case of a sensual description such as this, society is still non-physical, and it remains explanatory to one's own internal feelings. "Society" remains the object onto which this *"oceanic feeling"* is projected. And yet, even when designating society as the object of psychological projections, as we have argued for in the last chapter of this opuscule, a certain suspicion presents itself. We want to ask, *is society a mere expression of a desire?*—perhaps a goal, such that when *being one with the external world is absent*, we can point to "society!" for actions to guide solutions? The answer seems to be a resounding "yes". And in light of modern transportation and communication technologies, we should not be surprised that such a desire for *society as goal* is overly present in our *here* and *now*. No doubt, modern commerce presents us with a great need for such society—certainly when presented with exotic or otherwise foreign cultures. However, what is interesting and, at the same time, perhaps also seemingly perverse, is that the need for society is often less apparent in our own backyard. Yet, this is the location where *being as one with the external world* may also be strikingly absent—especially once we have been presented with a system of business and commerce which pulls us in the direction away from our locale. International big business is exciting, and, if so, we may find the need for society lacking on the local level. In such cases, we could say that it is more difficult to confront *the uncanny* than it is to confront *the exotic*. Despite this, and no matter

155

the case, this desire for society is relevant to our project at hand, whether as a resolution to uncanniness, to exoticness, or to some other aesthetic experience altogether. Therefore, throughout the rest of this chapter, let us see if we can save society, or *societas*, as a barometer by which to measure the successes and/or failures of our economic reforms.

In previous chapters, we had qualified αληθευειν as a motionless action—one which announces itself and, at the same time, demands a primordial reckoning. Furthermore, we designated the πολις as the "radius" of αληθευειν. Inasmuch, we should not be surprised that any description which fails to presence αληθευειν may at first appear as rather strange when measured against the πολις. And when that description appears to be located within the mouth of another human animal, it may present itself as amoral, or as the product of under-education and selfishness. But, in all honesty, we should ask ourselves, *why is this the case*? After all, it is not an encounter with the strange which encourages such psychological assessments. However, if we venture out towards our own psychological diagnosis, then it could be on account of a hostility towards disagreement. And what seems painfully obvious is that the spirit of progressivism is that which has bred a kind of playground for encounters with such hostilities. However, if we restrain ourselves from making any psychological diagnoses of our own—ones which may themselves encourage hostility— then we are granted access to a higher perspective. Recalling previous chapters, we remember that in the writings of the Ancient Greek philosophers, we find testaments to the experience of the δημος—the public. We can trace this experience through the testimony of the Western tradition, up to, and including, the philosophers of the twentieth century. We have taken Walter Lippman, John Dewey, and Martin

Heidegger as our examples at times throughout our development. Within this tradition, to be as δημιουργος (as that which produces the outward appearance of the world within the commerce of public uses of things and of communal life) is to be as δημος. What should be noted is that if we continue to understand democracy not from the perspective of top-down government administration, but in the sense of communal economy, then the production of the δημιουργος is, and can only ever be, a manifestation of ιδεα insofar as the δημιουργος is equally being as the δημος. That is to say, the ιδεα essentially belongs to *the people*. Therefore, the δημιουργος can only ever present the ιδεα through such production, being as one such instance of *the people*. Consequently, if the ιδεα is not of the δημος, then neither is the being of the producer as δημιουργος.

Following this explication of the δημιουργος and the δημος, and after having been presented with the pervasiveness of the public in the Western tradition, we can perhaps all-too easily understand the progressives and, specifically, their hostility towards disagreement. No doubt, there is a logical *sameness* apparent in this relationship, namely, δημιουργος to δημος. After all, to be as δημιουργος is to be as δημος. The progressive is guided logically—a logic which, if disrupted or outright broken, presents an incompressible picture of the world. Of course, this is true for the progressive just as much as it is for anyone else. But what is more?—it is all-too easy to fall into the kinds of assumptions which also plagued the Ancient Greeks—namely, that the phenomenon of the proximal human animal is, in most cases, always in its being as δημος. This assumption, then, gives rise to the expectation of similarity between all human animals, whether proximal or not. And this expectation then provides for the hostility towards disagreement between human animals. Of course, focusing on this point, we are reminded of our need to overcome the biases inherent within the Western tradition, biases that prioritize the human animal within its systems and teachings. After all, if we de-animate the being of δημιουργός as something tantamount to that of the δῆμος, then what becomes animate is exactly that which is common to both—namely, the common moment of the encounter, conditioned by the primordial *wheeling and dealing* which is itself grounded upon projection, within the radius which is the πόλις. The commonness of this encounter is present no matter if, whether or not, the encounter is accompanied by an uncanniness or by an exoticness, whether in the locale of our very own backyard or within a foreign country.

Of course, in sympathizing with the progressives, what should equally be admitted is that progressivism has not *only* taken up naïve appeals towards self-similarity, thereby being ignorant to all that is interesting and important in difference. The spirit of progressivism has also evolved alongside its own working solutions towards *societas*. Of course, these solutions are worth mentioning. We might find them useful in advancing towards our own prescriptions. On a very practical level, then, say within the management class, we find a celebration of deliberation and, above all else, human reason as the operating faculty towards decision—that moment of decision, then, suggests to the office manager that society has been achieved. However, while evidently healthy, there is also good reason for bringing this celebration into question. The Danish theologian, Hal Koch, championed as much. He understood that it was not decision, but deliberation itself which offered value. After all, deliberation secures the individual's rights over the terminality of the majority's decision. Therefore, Koch's conclusion is consistent with our investigations thus far. Deliberation, in a more robust sense, is a type of laboring, and labor is the political expression of both the moment of the encounter and the "venue" for truth. And yet, if we do decide to take up this *deliberation* as we advance towards our prescriptions in the remaining chapters ahead, then we should also be careful not to undermine the very nature of truth—a nature which is obscured by progressivism's decision, and one which may still be jeopardized because of deliberation.

Therefore, in order that we may, in good conscience, take up deliberation into our project to nurture truth and authenticity, we must also acknowledge that description is something which, by its very nature as disclosive of the phenomenal experience, could never be common among any set of human animals (or even agreed upon between them). Description is, after all, unique to each expression as it appears in the moment of the encounter. Inasmuch, any "agreement" on any one particular description could only "steal" that description from another. And while this may feel pedantic to those invested with the spirit of progressivism, it is exactly this spirit which has gone on to obscure genuine disclosure. Consider the common experience of the sunset. No matter how many times that experience has been had, the profundity of that experience could never be taken away. One's own description of that experience will forever be their own unique expression. No matter how convincing the scientist's common material description may be, if we wish to nurture truth, then we must resist submitting ourselves to such scientific nihilism. Recalling the first half of this opuscule, we remember that experience which we took as a prototype for grounding our economic reforms—that which was teased in the very first chapter of this opuscule:

the art museum. We remember that in works of art, we find not only a "safe space", but also a "safe time". It is not without reason that throughout the literature of our historical continuum, the ascetic hermit is regarded as one who is worthy of our ear. He is, after all, the one who listens to nature, and this time spent listening provides for a disposition more venerable than that presented by the fast-talking salesman. With this in mind, we understand that it is not deliberation and consensus which truth demands of us, nor is it even a *listening society* as the Scandinavian metamodernists have proposed—that is, at least, if we understand society as an exclusively human possibility. Instead, if we honor truth, and if we wish to nurture truth and authenticity in the emergent project, then truth demands of us a satisfying feedback loop relationship with all of nature. And so, if we wish to nurture truth and authenticity, then we must prescribe a freedom *for* deliberation, but not necessarily a deliberation with other human animals in each and every case. We will keep this insight with us as we proceed into our economic reform prescriptions.

Of course, this lonesome subjectivation of description, as something *"unique to each expression"*, may also provoke another concern. This is a concern which we have inherited by way of the epistemic tradition—that which we can frame as a *solipsistic* worldview. However, the solipsistic concern is undoubtedly a consequence of the primordial *actio* of episteme—an *actio* which continually seeks to satisfy our need for security by way of domination and the apprehension of a totality. This includes even the somewhat perverse apprehension of another's mind. If we do not get caught up in knowing another person's innermost desires (the quest of science and the stuff of science fiction novels) and instead look at the phenomena which present themselves over in experience, then the estrangement of fellow "man" becomes less articulate—if intelligible at all. Beyond the paradigm of absolute knowledge, the obstacle of a *me* meeting a *you* disappears,

> "We don't feel lonely in our unique experience, or left out of the ineffable experiences of others. We are already confident that we are completed by others, and that the sum total of human experience resides in the sum total of human experience—that it can never be captured or known by anyone or by any one."

We have repeated this passage here by way of the previously mentioned report, *Open to Participate*, by Bonnitta Roy. The *"captured"* of which she speaks directs our attention to the "apprehension" of the often-sought intellectual narrative which tells the story of a "oneness"—of a "humanity"—a story which appeals to a sense of wholesomeness, or belonging. However, what is required for truth to be consequent and disclosive, as well as for it to fulfil its nature in *being projective*, is difference. It is exactly at the "fault line" of difference between the being as δημιουργος and the αληθευειν of the πολις where we can find the unique truth of the moment and, thereby, novel value creation also. Inasmuch, it seems obvious that any reformational prescriptions which could bring us closer to an economy founded upon αληθευειν demands a quite dramatic mantra: we must forgo our position as a Western δημιουργος directed towards his or her people—towards "the human race"; we must forgo those attempts to prove our humanity when presented with uncanniness or exoticness; and, we must not flatter displays of outrage when our humanity has been offended, like when we feel an urge to name-call—"Nazi!"—being just one example, of course. To put it crudely, we must celebrate the expectation that when we open our mouths, we are also met with difference.

In announcing an expectation of difference, it should also be said that we are, furthermore, not interested in escalating tensions at the moment of the disclosure either. We must remember that the truth of any one description present in the moment of the encounter could only ever be "proven" in the fact that it provides traction, and thus propels the moment forward into the next moment. Insofar as this is the case, only together, in each moment, in the very forum of the encounter, with the entirety of the phenomena of experience (and not merely alongside the human animal), will the truth then be revealed as the truth which has always been and which could never have been otherwise. Consequently, and insofar as we are not interested in any forms of forced alignment at the moment of the encounter, we must equally celebrate the expectation that some descriptions will have to remain *yet to be decided on*. Of course, this does not mean that we should be *eager* to shove those descriptions aside, into some dark corner which we could call "the undecided", never to be revisited again. Actually, quite the opposite—we should be prepared to revisit them whenever the need arises. However, what we should expect is that, in most cases, once any particular description has presented itself as *yet to be decided on*, then what is likely at issue is not the truth of the description itself, but rather the relevance of that description to the project at hand. And, that is to say, any description which presents itself as *yet to be decided on*, will not have shown its priority within the πολις, once measured against the projection which has drawn us together into that radius. And so, for example, in the 1990s, we found a Christian πολις, which presented a description of the world as "intelligently designed". Likewise, we found an atheistic πολις presenting a seemingly contrary position—"biological evolution". Yet, regarding the American people as a whole, or rather, *the American πολις*, a decision on either description, whether "intelligent design" or "biological evolution", could not be taken. And consequently, it was left as *yet to be decided on*, and it remains so until this very day.

With this said, perhaps it is now becoming clear that our project to nurture truth and authenticity does, after all, demand quite a few starting conditions of its own. And if those conditions are not met, then we must encourage some healthy skepticism, even within ourselves and towards our very own project. It could be said that if we honor truth, then *truth demands something of us too.* Consider, for example, that beyond an expectation of difference, truth also demands that the moment of the encounter, as the locus of authenticity, should also be characterized by something resembling audacity. Of course, audacity here does not mean arrogance, or any other epistemological bullishness whatsoever. To be sure, the audacity which we refer to here is not *personal*; it is not *psychological*. We have attempted to leave behind such individual-subjectivity in the first half of this opuscule. Rather, the audacity which we refer to here regards the character of the encounter. It refers to the character of each and every one who is present at the encounter. Such an audacity does, we must admit, provide fertile ground for a spirit of a more experimental description—a spirit which can then, in turn, provide for the unique (and therefore most appropriate) articulation within the moment. Only that type of articulation can project us towards the next moment after that. Therefore, while audacity may seem like a perverse disposition demanded of truth, it is nonetheless required for respecting truth, and inasmuch, is required for respecting every other human animal who is present at the encounter and who shares in the pursuit of having the truth. Therefore, it is through audacity that we might *have* belonging. Belonging is, of course, founded upon a condition which each of us are overly familiar with. It is only on account of this familiarity that we can understand the condition at all. Inasmuch, this drive to have belonging is indicative of a *belonging as condition* to which we wish to return. Returning is bound up with removing obstruction and revealing that which has always been. Acknowledging this return releases us from the complexification or reductionism which objects such as "the global" or "humanity" force upon us—those objects which the spirit of progressivism abuses. Inasmuch, we understand that "returning" characterizes any genuine prescriptions for resolving alienation and estrangement.

Now, in heeding this general movement towards *return*, we must also be careful not to narrow the depth of possible description. Of course, we must reach whatever depth is necessary in order to make this return. Therefore, if we must draw definitions in order to reach an appropriate depth at the moment of the encounter, then it must be done by *localizing*. Only by narrowing breadth instead of limiting depth can we begin to honor that unknowable ruler and *God from Below*—the very subject of our economic reform proposal—namely, *discourse*. This then indicates the first of our prescriptions, even if it is quite a "light" prescription at that. If we proceed in this way towards *the below*, and if we heed the demands of truth in doing so, then we just might be allowed to meet the progressive, such that we can mutually take up *society as goal*. Of course, our society is not to be understood as the "forum" where truth is to be decided. We are not suggesting mob rule; this much should be clear. Rather, our society is something of *a fellowship* or *an association*, perhaps an *alliance* or a *union*. Explicitly, it is *societas*. And much like our "audacity" as mentioned above, the "association" and "alliance" of *societas* is not psychological; nor could it ever be observed in any particular person who is present at the encounter. Rather, *societas* describes the character of the encounter. *Societas* is an engagement with the commerce of the moment. In this way, when we speak of *societas*, we are also speaking of that which the Ancient Greeks referred to as κοινωνια—a word which serves as a placeholder for the joint share which anyone (and any thing) present has in the encounter. Only as something like *this* could we take up society as our barometer for the success or failure of our economic reform. And we would do well to do so.

With all of this said, we may now proceed. You could say that only now, after twelve chapters, and by way of our considerations with regards to language, history, and the phenomenal experience, have we earned the right of passage. The following remaining chapters will present prescriptions for resolving the contention between discourse and truth as announced in the previous chapter. We will firstly look at prototypical activity which is drawing new definitions for governing the πολις. No doubt, these definitions offer a novel space which we might be able to reproduce in other locations, and in doing so, come to satisfy that which has been lost while being coddled in the market, and in being estranged from public office and state governance.

However, before we proceed, let us take the opportunity for one last reflection here in this chapter. After all, we must admit that our above considerations about the Christian πολις, the atheistic πολις, and the American πολις, have also allowed for an opportunity to consider another phenomenon—an opportunity which may prove no less relevant to our project at hand. Consider the fact that the phenomenal experience consists of many various, and often competing, projects. Of course, our various "radiuses" do not have definite boundaries, such that we could measure them as if they were physical objects. Therefore, it should be obvious that projection, too, often mixes and blurs; and, inasmuch, the objects and tools taken up into those projects also mix and blur. Therefore, we can expect something of a *repoliticalization* of objects and tools—from one project to another—and we can expect a confounding of linguistic objects, especially. Insofar as this is the case, let us now consider this phenomenon of "repoliticalization" more thoroughly, as is fitting to do and especially so here in this chapter, since we have undertaken a consideration of sociological concerns while also attempting to answer them with *first economics* philosophy. After all, if our philosophy of primordial economics is to prove itself useful within the emergent project, and thereby lead us towards answers for nurturing truth and authenticity, then it must not only account for the sociological problems, but it must answer them in a more satisfying way than does the logic which takes society and its values as the first and principal objects of study. No subsequent chapters will allow us this reflection.

Therefore, in order to consider *repoliticalization* more thoroughly, let us consider the activism championed under the banner of Black Lives Matter following the death of George Floyd, and let us furthermore understand this activism as a reaction to evidence of extreme measures taken by police forces ("police brutality") against those who have been either identified by ethnologists as black, or self-identified as such. If we are to understand this Black Lives Matter activism in this way, then we can say that the object *race* was "repoliticalized" through the Black Lives Matter movement—insofar as race became an issue outside of "police brutality". And while we can admit that a repoliticalization of objects and tools may produce novel elucidation, it might also create conditions ripe for hostility. Consider that even prior to the activism following the death of George Floyd, Robin DiAngelo's book *White Fragility* had empowered many—her diagnosis for this fragility was "white guilt", and other such psychological artifacts. However, at the same time, even if "white fragility" and "white guilt" were felt as true among a certain set of human animals, we should not shunt aside the suffering which any "whites" may then have experienced when confronted with such psychological diagnoses. Likewise, we should not shunt aside any anxiety which may have been experienced in the face of the violent measures taken by Black Lives Matter activists. To do so would be quite inhumane, after all. The evidence for this suffering is quite sufficient, in any case. Repoliticalization, as an extrapolation towards the universal, is a move which has historically conditioned hostility; therefore, we should expect that it will continue to do so in the future. Insofar as this is the case, and if we wish to nurture truth and authenticity, *and* if we are to remain true to our first prescription (namely, to heed to the general movement towards return, and to narrow breadth rather than limit depth) then we should take caution with repoliticalization. Briefly, we can mention one alternative to repoliticalization already now. One alternative would be to create novel objects—both tools and language—from within the radius which is the πολις. After all, the project is that which has already drawn us together into a single projection. This alternative would hold, even if the radius of our project is something as broad as the American πολις.

# Drawing New Definitions for Governance

We are used to thinking of governance jurisdictions as Russian matryoshka dolls—one jurisdiction within another parent jurisdiction, *ad infinitum*. The person lives in the city, the city within the municipality, the municipality within the state, and finally, the state within a federation. Yet, this monological succession of governance is an oversimplification. It does not exhaust our entire roster of governance conditions. No doubt, each one of us is also bound by the governance of our tradition, that social governance which is written into the very fabric of our discourse, that which is today only idolized by the word *nation*. Of course, today, what is likely more elucidating are the marketing regions defined by corporate marketeers. For sure, marketeers invest in commercial regions which do abide by local state legislations, but their campaigns are neither wholly nor exclusively defined by that legislation. Without a doubt, we have been delivered over to a disposition of *poly-governance*—including, but not limited to, administrative, social, and commercial marketing governance. And while these qualifications of governance are so broad that we could never escape such "poly-governance", it is exactly from within the poly-governance of our everyday commerce that we have been met with the contention between discourse and truth. In this chapter, we will use the metaphysical architectonic established over the preceding chapters to identify certain political activities, activities which have drawn new definitions within the governance of the factual lives of real people—definitions which promise to return truth back to proximity, such that we can honor that primordial, primal, and prime governor—that which we have called *discourse*—in the emergent project.

Let us now return to the historical narrative of truth as we left it at the closing of the first half of this opuscule. Recalling chapter six will help us to remember the conclusion to that narrative. In that chapter, we had made it clear that in the *here* and *now*, in our *"time between worlds"*, liberal values have shown themselves to be a vehicle for the primordial *actio* of episteme—both by way of legislative domestication (that which we named *governance as law*), and also by way of market economy. We likewise stated, implicitly, that *governance as law* and market economy have not proven themselves to be satisfactory in projecting us towards our longer-term horizons. We took as our evidence the previously cited testimony from United States Advisor on Climate Change, James Gustav Speth. However, we could just as well call to the many critiques which have been waged against capital. No doubt, any of the following would do: the critique of "the global elite", or "the one-percent", or "the deep state". We could likewise call to the many critiques which have been waged against the contributors to the World Economic Forum, especially with their calls for a "Great Reset". And, we could equally call towards any one of the various critiques which have been waged against the techno and social media robber barons of the early-third millennium. Each of these are a testament to the dissatisfaction with our current projection towards our longer horizons.

Of course, what should be clear, given this short list, is that the critique of the subjectivist paradigm has generally been waged against "neoliberalism" and the economic description which we know as capitalism. This means that the critique of the subjectivist paradigm has not been waged against the subjectivist paradigm itself, which includes liberalism (whether we are, again, speaking of the liberation of the individual-subject or the identity-subject). Of course, throughout our narrative of the historical economy of truth, we had not joined in the critique of capital, nor did we choose to animate any of the previously mentioned conspiracy theories. Even now, we do not intend to critique capital, nor any other economic system by which material is managed. Instead, we wish to use our diagnosis of the essential economy of *parse to transcend*, and of the primordial *actio* of episteme, and of the subjectivist paradigm itself in order to prescribe *primordial economic reform* by proposing mechanisms of economic democracy. Despite this, we can expect the critics of capital to join in the appreciation of our proposal. Obviously, any worldly governance which fails to take into account a primordial *discourse* and a primordial *projection* can only exacerbate the symptoms of modernization—namely, alienation, rootlessness, estrangement, and apathy. We understand these as the principal challenges in the emergent project. We also understand that these challenges, if addressed, would likewise address many auxiliary challenges too. We can even venture to include the aforementioned challenge of ecological sustainability among them. Therefore, we conclude thusly: what is demanded of future governance, if it is to be a *humane governance* within the emergent project, is the execution of what might be called *governance as projection*, along with its respective mechanisms.

Today, truth demands from us *project governance*. Therefore, if at the conclusion of this opuscule, and after considering all that is presented, we do decide to heed to our concerns regarding our dissatisfaction with the disclosure of truth coupled with our dissatisfaction with our current state of liberation for authenticity (while also wishing to heed to our ideal of democracy as a form of governance in which truth is an object of concern for the human animal), then we are, without a doubt, directed towards project governance. By way of such governance, we should expect the proximal workspace of *wheeling and dealing* (that which we have qualified as the "forum" of truth) to recover truth from its seemingly exclusive service to industrial-liberation as *the positive fact*. That is, we should expect that from within the proximal workspace, we will meet with a redemption of truth, understood and activated in its nature as *disclosive* and *projective*. This means that if we choose to activate our prescriptions for nurturing truth and authenticity as we go forward, then we should also expect that from within the proximal workspace, the dichotomy between *public truth* and that often sought *inner truth* will have collapsed onto one another. And this means, explicitly, that we will have stripped truth from technocracy, in which industry experts are invested with the responsibility over truth in its intellectual form. However, this also means that we will have stripped truth from the mob, namely *society*, which has historically been known to take control over truth through force. Inasmuch, we should expect nothing short of a reunion of truth and our everyday commerce. Of course, at this point in our development, it is yet to be decided if such governance jurisdiction could be established within our existing democratic institutions, within our existing market economy, or a combination of these two. Perhaps in the near future, we will find such jurisdiction arising somewhere else altogether. Though, for the time being, we must suspend our desire for any answers which conform to our current infrastructure. Furthermore, we should not burden ourselves such that our search for nascent *governance as projection* political activity results in being somewhat restricted. Let us now take our first steps and venture onwards into that search.

Roughly a decade ago, Southern Europe gave rise to several grassroots urban-based projects defined by a returning socialist ideology from the nineteenth century: *municipalism*. In 2016, Luigi De Magistris, mayor of Naples, remarked that these new municipalist movements had offered, *"an absolute novelty in the institutional and political panorama: that between civil society, social movements and local institutions there exists a relation under construction"*. No doubt, De Magistris' tripartite *"civil society"*, *"social movement"*, and *"local institutions"* calls towards the proximal. What we find particularly interesting is that by way of urban-based infrastructural projects, these municipalist movements manifested something of a *prefigurative* approach to political activity—an approach not *pre* in the developmental sense, but one which is instead a constant *pre-configuration* as the *figuration* forever lies in an unknown future, perhaps to only ever be described in history books. Repeating what was said by an anonymous representative of the Naples-based municipalist movement, Massa Critica, we read testimony to the spiritual motivations of these activists,

> "[Municipalism] is not a battle for ourselves, for our identity—we are communist, we are anarchist, we

173

> are…No. [Municipalism] is a battle directly from the people. For example, I fight for the hospital, I fight for commons, I fight for water. I fight for these single rights. I fight in a near, near way, for some rights where normal people are directly involved."

This quote has been pulled from an article titled *Beyond the Local Trap: New Municipalism and the Rise of the Fearless Cities* by Bertie Russell, published in 2019. What should be noted, then, is that if we retroactively classify these movements as *prefigurative*, then they also present themselves as something of a negation of all previous "configured" political activity. Yet, we must not be mistaken, that negation is a *positive* characteristic. After all, it is only from a *post-liberal* position (and that is to say, a negation of liberalism) that any political activity can move beyond liberalism's *battle of selfishness*—beyond Black Lives Matter and white nationalism, feminism and LGBTQ+ activism. Insofar as this is the case, these new municipalist movements had offered Southern Europe a novel canvas for truth from out of the ruins of liberalism's epistemological warfare—beyond the weaponizing of identity outright. Furthermore, we can say that this negation is not merely for the sake of recruitment into a new "post-liberal" ideology. For sure, that negation must remain as a negation, indefinitely. Otherwise, in becoming definite, any prefigurative political activity would cease to be prefigurative political activity and become a static *prefigurativism* instead. For this reason alone, if no other, we must consider further the municipalist movement as we progress towards our economic reform proposal. After all, this political activity seems to promise a venue for the primordial "action" of *αληθεύειν*, beyond epistemological comportment. And how fitting that it has animated the city in doing so?!

Of course, at the same time, we must also admit that taking up such a post-liberal position may simply feel apolitical to those possessed by a spirit for equality and minority rights. At its worst, a post-liberal position may lead us towards institutional conservatism. After all, within the state's political commerce, identity has always been an effective tool for swaying infrastructural investment. Recently, we find this *identity as tool* taken up in movements with agendas extraneous to what is on offer through the infrastructure inherited by way of colonization and patriarchy. Surely it is apparent in social justice activism. Therefore, we can expect objections to post-liberalism, even to prefigurative political activity, and perhaps even to municipalism too. However, we can also remove those objections from their home in contemporary political activism and, therefore, perhaps place those objections into a more rational debate—this is easily done, after all. We only need to consider the fact that identity has been a part of human civilization since long before the formation of liberalism's legislative power. No doubt, the flags of nations signaled *friend* from *enemy* in the commerce of battlefield warfare. *Identity as tool* can be traced back to long before the black flags were raised in the Abbasid Caliphate. Therefore, any prefigurative political activity, whether post-liberal or not, and as epistemically ignorant as it might seem, may simply strike any one of us as irrational. That is to say, we may not be able to psychologically rationalize prefigurative political activity on account of our historical records—despite the testimony we read from the municipalist movement as it stands today. However, while all of this is historically apparent, it is just that. We can be sure that the use of identity as tool in the commerce of political economy can only belong to a past historical timeline. After all, at this particular moment, the future is yet to be decided upon. That is not trivial. It is not said to be patronizing. What is relevant for us *here* and *now*, in considering the post-liberal position as *the* position of pre-figurative political activity, is to picture for ourselves exactly how reasoning works from within the post-liberal position. Specifically, it will be interesting for us to consider how to reason with those issues which we are accustomed to thinking of as liberal issues, but are, all the same, issues which we would likely wish to carry with us into the emergent project. As an example, we could take up that collection of issues which fall under the banner of women's rights. These issues are, after all, real-world issues which we will likely not abandon as we go forward in reforming the economy. Therefore, let us take up women's rights as our example for elucidating reasoning from within the post-liberal position. Let us, furthermore, consider women's rights from the abortion debate, and specifically by way of the pro-choice argument. (Of course, in taking up this argument, it should be said that abortion is not especially important to a post-liberal position; nevertheless, we will use the pro-choice argument, as it will allow us an example of how reasoning works from within the post-liberal position.)

Firstly then, we must acknowledge that the pro-choice argument explicitly takes for granted the objects, *freedom* and *choice*. Of course, objects such as these are often encountered as immutable and irrefutable. However, this does not mean that they are. Freedom and choice are often argued for on the presumption of the metaphysical object, *free will*. And much like *luck, destiny, "social power"*, and *"economic competition"*, "free will" too is an object used to explain causal occurrences and phenomena. Furthermore, and insofar as free will is in some relationship to the physical world, yet falls outside the domain of scientific explanation, we can say that it is *occult*. Therefore, free will is an object belonging to the *causal-occult* metaphysical category. Of course, we should not use this category pejoratively. However, this category does help us to identify the projects which free will has historically served. Free will is, for us today, a residue which we have inherited by way of our epistemological heritage—specifically, through the prioritization of "man" in the economy of the πολις. Yet, in acknowledging the primordial origins of the world—that which we have identified as discourse—objects such as an individual's free will and freedom cannot exist for us. After all, any individual-subject is forever subjected to that which we have identified as our *subiectum*—the primordial *wheeling and dealing discourse with nature*. And while a loss of free will may sound quite dramatic, in practice, it simply means we have no use for *that causal explanation*.

What follows then, in acknowledging discourse as the foundation for the world, is that we also lose the privilege for any reasoning which follows from an individual's free will and freedom and along with those explanatory objects also goes the pro-choice argument. All the same, we still have not answered for ourselves how post-liberal reasoning works. Let us proceed to do that now. And let us do so, again, by way of the pro-choice argument, but this time in a more round-about way. Consider that once we have explicitly and intellectually acknowledged that free will has lost any explanatory power, then we will have also circumvented those problems which arise from restricting the right of any gendered man from having a say over the legalization or the illegalization of abortion among his people. After all, without free will, it is logically impossible for any man to ever have a say over any woman's will. Instead, presuming that any one particular man, just as any woman, is produced of our primordial *wheeling and dealing,* then he has (in his being as *always having been there*) already contributed to the decision on the issue, and will continue to in any future moments. Of course, at the same time, none of this is to say that, from within either prefigurative political activity or from a post-liberal position, anyone must be insensitive to the well-being of any woman with a life-threatening pregnancy. Abortion, if taken as a health issue, may very well fall within the program of any infrastructural project. However, as an issue of infrastructure and medical welfare, any decision to publicly fund abortion cannot be assumed as universal, say, on account of human rights. Instead, this is a decision which can only be taken by any local peoples, again, by both men and women, as an act of projecting towards *the good* for themselves. It is only by taking up a primordial projection, as the very foundation for *all* value creation, that a post-liberal reasoning can begin. Of course, we cannot exercise similar treatments on every issue which we might wish to animate in the emergent project; however, perhaps the above analysis on the pro-choice argument will help to guide the reader in understanding how other avenues and forms of reasoning might follow, once we have abandoned liberal reasoning and are standing firmly with a post-liberal position instead.

With all of that said, let us now close on the post-liberal position. In doing so, we should make it clear that any promotion of prefigurative political activity is not tantamount to a promotion of ignorance towards any one particular real-world concern. Again, and taking the municipalist movement as our example, we should not overlook the fact that because these movements had operated outside of existing structures, they had thusly appealed to those agents with agendas extraneous to what was on offer through colonization and patriarchy—that is, they had appealed specifically to women and minorities. Following the successes of the

Southern European movements, municipalist political activity was tried in locations across both North and South America. In recalling what was said by a representative of Argentina's Ciudad Futura, we thus read of a spiritual motivation beyond liberalism's justice, rights, law, surveillance, and punishment. In their own words, "[Municipalism had offered] *the possibility of constructing a new kind of power in society which is precisely in the hands of ordinary people*". A "*local governance, which allows for proximity*" and, as stated by the representative of Ciudad Futura, "*allows us to project our experience on another scale*".

Without a doubt, this "*new kind of power*" of which the representative speaks is not a power which results from merely stripping power from out of the hands of the existing authorities and replacing it into "*the hands of ordinary people*". After all, a transposition of social power could never come to deanimate domesticative epistemological warfare. Instead, these words testify to the fact that, through infrastructural urban-based projects, the municipalist approach towards politics had encouraged a confrontation with that primordial *actio ἀληθεύειν*—a confrontation which, in the representative's own words, "*allows us to project our experience on another scale*". Therefore, if for no other reason, we should bring this political movement into our consideration as we advance towards prescriptions for economic reform. And while we have only covered this movement briefly, here in this chapter, any reader is encouraged to research for themselves the new municipalist movement further. (The previously mentioned article, *Beyond the Local Trap: New Municipalism and the Rise of the Fearless Cities*, by Bertie Russell, is a recommended resource. At the time of writing this chapter, the article is available for free download online.)

Now, of course, at the same time, this does not mean we cannot be critical of such a program for political activity on other accounts—and we should be. After all, there is one hesitation which strikes us immediately. While municipalism offers a novel venue beyond state/federal infrastructure, we should also be critical of a continued celebration of the city as a flagship venue for human commerce. Such a celebration harbors residue left over from internationalism primarily—namely, a spirit of commerce and cosmopolitanism—from New York to London, Paris and Tokyo. This is a spirit which has exacerbated the contention between urban and provincial communities. Therefore, we must say already now, that if we are to prescribe a municipalist political strategy, then we must also champion something of a *regionalization* which might overcome that contention. No doubt, continuing with an economy which produces "red states" and "blue states" can offer little to a project concerned with establishing the conditions for authenticity. However, we are also not the first in our tradition to recognize this. If we return to E.F. Schumacher's *Small is Beautiful*, we can thus recall the announcement of a *"becoming existence"*— one which is characterized by a work which *"gives a man a chance to utilise and develop his faculties"*, and *"enables man to overcome his egocentredness by joining with other people in a common task"*. Of course, here we cannot think of *"common task"* as merely performing the same exercise. Picking apples from the same tree. Turning the same screws on the assembly line. A common task is that which is *commonly projected*. Schumacher acknowledged that for such a becoming existence, founded upon a common projection, *"there is need for a 'cultural structure' just as there is need for an 'economic structure'"*. *"Each region, ideally speaking, requires some sort of inner cohesion"*, with a capital city serving as a center. His program for a regionalization is equally a *bio*-regionalization—one in which the metropolitan center does not serve the international identity, but is instead a canvas for the cultural-economic region. Of course, *bio* here does not refer to *genetics* or some other narrow signification which might carry over from the scientific industries. The existence which springs forth through such *"becoming"* is life itself—it is *life-logical*. Biological.

Having turned towards Schumacher's *Small is Beautiful*, we have, as in the first half of this opuscule, accrued a collection of nice-sounding words. A *life-logical bioregionalism*. This gets us thinking even towards ecology. These associations are not accidental. Our guiding method—that is, our vantage point from which we *have* the world, namely *phenomenology*—had already prepared us for such ecological thinking. Not only has the human animal collapsed onto non-human animals and machines, but by way of our phenomenological commitment, "man" has also collapsed under the entirety of the phenomenal experience. Inasmuch, we value each equally. No doubt, upon encountering this thought, we have reason to be proud. To flatter ourselves. However, at the same time, we should not proceed all-too happily. After all, it could be argued that the anthropocentric worldview and epistemological comportment towards the phenomenal experience is, after all, that which might save Mother Earth. Yet, there is a depth worth elucidating in our approach. A depth which tells us that following our phenomenological commitment leads to robust solutions. Following the precedent established with Schumacher, we are encouraged to *fantasize* such robustness. We animate that robustness over any merely numerous solutions. Undoubtedly, fantasy is highly alluring. It calls for submersion—"an exploration of the universe". In anticipating a future economy which addresses modernization's alienation, rootlessness, estrangement, and apathy, we are doing futurism. Belonging to this future economy are civil works programs. We imagine these programs not merely tasked with the construction of material infrastructure (bridges, streets, or power plants), but also with the aesthetic expressions of that infrastructure—those which, today, we find reserved for the fine arts of yesterday, and are still present in poetry, literature, and philosophy. Our imagination calls forth Franklin D. Roosevelt's New Deal, including the Federal Arts Program, the aesthetics of which also celebrate *labor, regionalism,* and *ecology*—themes which announced themselves in art deco murals found on United States Post Office walls, still to this very day. It is here, in this moment of our fantasy, that we turn towards the second political activity which we wish to spotlight in this chapter. Now, the United States military is perhaps an unlikely venue for bioregional *governance as projection* infrastructure. All the same, we are about to highlight an infrastructure where state commerce and civil projects have remained in union, and as such, preserve that primordial harmony with nature—a communion which is found in a marriage of **belief** and **action**. We now look towards the United States Army; specifically, the third division of the engineering formation devoted to civil engineering projects. But before we begin, perhaps we require a few conditioning remarks. After all, in announcing the United States *military*, we may already feel an atomic disgust in response. Perhaps a feeling of betrayal on behalf of our efforts so far. Therefore, let it be said *clearly* that we are not interested in any self-subjection to the democratically weak outlet for authenticity—authoritarianism. Our fantasies about bioregionalism do not include any uniformed federal officers and soldiers terraforming local regions according to the orders of a remote commander-in-chief. Let us remind ourselves that civic engagement, as grounded in αληθεύειν, is motivated by primordial inspiration, lust, and desire for engagement which we find at the locus of creation—something which we have come to know as authenticity. We understand that the ideal of democracy requires a civic engagement which can no longer be satisfied by mere voting alone, but only by a cultivation of *authenticity* in the hands of artists, designers, engineers, statesmen, economists, and philosophers. Let us also, therefore, take this opportunity to say that any prescriptions for nurturing truth and authenticity which come out of a consideration of the United States military could never be for the sake of a nation's "greater good". Even John F. Kennedy's "*Ask not what your country can do for you, but what you can do for your country*" has no place in our fantasy. Likewise, any civic engagement that is grounded in αληθεύειν could never carry over any residual hangovers from the period of liberal market policy, a period which was characterized by a discomforting elitism and privileged volunteer work. As we argued in chapter six of this opuscule, producing for one's livelihood can have nothing to do with selfishness such that sacrifice could become a virtue. One could never sacrifice their own personal commerce for their people—they are themselves, through that commerce, "*We, the people*". Contrary to such virtues of sacrifice, we are interested in an infrastructure for enabling communion, and one that extends beyond the mere ballot.

With these qualifying remarks, we now proceed to an exploration of the United States military, firstly, in that it offers a governance jurisdiction beyond the state/federal *governance as law* canvas. Today, the United States Army Corps of Engineers (USACE) is the largest owner-operator of hydroelectric plants in the United States. It owns and operates 75 plants—24% of US hydropower capacity.

The Corps of Engineers also preserves, restores, creates, or enhances approximately 38,700 acres (157,000,000 m2) of wetlands annually. In addition, the Corps of Engineers is the nation's principal provider of outdoor recreation, with more than 368 million visits annually to 4,485 sites. What is more, the Corps is committed to small business. Each year, approximately one-third of all contract dollars are obligated to small businesses, small disadvantaged businesses, disabled veteran-owned small businesses, women-owned small businesses, historically underutilized business zones, and historically black colleges and universities. And yet, it is not merely these facts which hold promise—it is the Corps of Engineers' divisions as defined by North American watershed regions. The Corps of Engineers is organized geographically into eight permanent divisions, one provisional division, one provisional district, and one research command that reports directly to the HQ. Within each division of the Corp, there are several districts.

Lakes and Ohio River Division (LRD), located in Cincinnati. Covers 355,300 square miles (920,000 km2), and portions of seventeen states. Its seven districts are located in Buffalo, Chicago, Detroit, Louisville, Nashville, Pittsburgh, and Huntington, West Virginia.

Mississippi Valley Division (MVD), located in Vicksburg, Mississippi. Covers 370,000 square miles (960,000 km2), and portions of twelve states bordering the Mississippi River. Its six districts are located in St. Paul, Minnesota, Rock Island, Illinois, St. Louis, Memphis, Vicksburg, and New Orleans.

North Atlantic Division (NAD), headquartered at Fort Hamilton in Brooklyn, New York. Its six districts are located in New York City, Philadelphia, Baltimore, Norfolk, Concord, Massachusetts, and an overseas mission to provide engineering, construction, and project management services to the US European Command and US Africa Command, headquartered in Wiesbaden, Germany.

Northwestern Division (NWD), located in Portland, Oregon. Covers nearly 1,000,000 square miles (2,600,000 km2) in all or parts of fourteen states. Its five districts are located in Omaha, Portland, Seattle, Kansas City, and Walla Walla. NWD has 35% of the total Corps of Engineers' water storage capacity and 75% of the total hydroelectric capacity.

South Atlantic Division (SAD), located in Atlanta. Covers all or parts of six states. Its five districts are located in Wilmington, North Carolina, Charleston, South Carolina, Savannah, Jacksonville, and Mobile. SAD manages the Everglades Restoration Project—the largest single environmental restoration project in the world.

South Pacific Division (SPD), located in San Francisco. Covers all or parts of seven states. Its four districts are located in Albuquerque, Los Angeles, Sacramento, and San Francisco.

Southwestern Division (SWD), located in Dallas. Covers all or part of seven states. Its four districts are located in Little Rock, Tulsa, Galveston, and Fort Worth. SWD's recreation areas are the most visited in USACE, with more than 11,400 miles (18,300 km) of shoreline and 1,172 recreation sites.

Additionally, the **Pacific Ocean Division** (POD), located at Fort Shafter, Hawaii, reaches across 12 million square miles of the Pacific Ocean. It goes from the Arctic Circle all the way to American Samoa below the equator, across the International Date Line, and into Asia. Its four districts are located in Japan; Seoul, South Korea; Anchorage, Alaska; and Honolulu. Furthermore, the **Transatlantic Division** (TAD), located in Winchester, Virginia, supports Federal programs and policies overseas.

No doubt, a map is a guide. Through such a guide, we encounter a temporal-spatial manifold. The manifold presents a landscape, and within this landscape, we discover a realm of possible activity. The mechanical and social topography of the world announces itself in a map, and we are pulled through the possibilities within. A map is not merely for those traversing geological terrain. A map captures and captivates us. **A map moves the soul.** What appears as profoundly lacking is a map for future governance beyond the state/federal and global market canvases. And while it may be unlikely that watershed regions are those which will bring together a bioregion as a jurisdiction for *governance as projection*, the Corps of Engineers offers an exercise for the soul. We should not be afraid of allowing ourselves the freedom to explore the realms of time and space which open up to us in the division maps.

In an effort to produce a book which is both affordable and accessible, we have chosen not to reproduce the full colour-maps here on these pages. This decision has allowed us to keep the manufacturing costs of this product low, so that we can then pass on those savings to you, the reader, for your benefit. Therefore, in order to complete this exercise, please open the camera on your smart device. Next, point your device at the QR code, and wait for the camera to recognize and then scan the code. Click the banner or notification when it appears on your screen; the maps will load automatically.

Localizing the Horizons of Projection

Today, we stand within a vision. We have been brought to this moment with the understanding that to describe the human animal as merely an empire builder (as that animal who apprehends, oversees, surmounts, and dominates) is to describe him from the "exterior"—scientifically. That is, sociologically. Such an approach towards "man" produces "the modern". The modern ideal is *utopia*, such that "man", this particular "modern man", is to be liberated. Those invested with this ideal seek nothing short of a "uni-verse". As manifested within politics, the modern is totalitarian. Therefore, the warfare of modern political theory is conducted by way of packaged deals— liberalism vs nationalism, or capitalism vs communism— such that today, we understand the victor of the ideological war as a United States-led liberalism, built upon capital and market economics, and partnered with social welfare programs. Yet, this understanding is something of a simplification. This becomes apparent when considering the variety of platforms on offer during the United States Democratic Party's 2020 presidential primaries—

where we find appeals to even nationalism alive and well in, for example, Pete Buttigieg's *National Service Plan*. Furthermore, if this plan were to be coupled with Bernie Sanders' *Medical for All* national health insurance program, then you might say that even the United States has, as belonging to its possible future, National Socialism— at least as things stood in 2020. Of course, the spirit for liberalism is certainly alive and well in these platforms. No one there is proposing fascist political economy in which the democratic institutions, education, news media, and market are subject to coercion from the elected party. However, even when the liberal spirit is explicitly evident (for example, in the gun-toting American), we can still imagine circumstances which would call for emergency action without deliberation—an exercise we might think of as authoritarian. Inasmuch, it is naïve to think that liberalism won, such that its rivals had been defeated. We must admit that each and every ideal, from liberalism and social welfare to nationalism and authoritarianism, are all present in the *here* and *now*. Of course, equipped with this understanding, we must admit that, unfortunately for those who laughed at and disregarded any claims that "true communism has not been tried"— well, neither has true liberalism. *True liberalism* as a true liberation from governance could only be realized as a utopia once man was free from any so-called governor, save his own-most moral compass, understood as "the law of Nature". However, it is yet to be decided if a form of governance utilizing such a one-sided ideal would be desirable or not. After all, we would likely call this *anarchism*; and even as the liberal spirit runs through us today, presented with a globalizing market economy, there is reason for why the name anarchy inspires feelings of disgust. We are not in possession of the conditions necessary for this type of governance. We do not have reason for it. In today's economy, *anarchy* is irrational. Therefore, it *performs* as negation. Punk culture is, for example, thoroughly *postmodern.*

Standing here in the liminal *here* and *now*—in this *"time between worlds"*—the icons of modernization have come into question. We stand not only above modern aesthetics, but equally above the postmodern antithesis—that which we understand as an expression of the same primordial *actio,* episteme. The residue of modernization's epistemological comportment are reminders of the modern ideal's totalitarian and imperialist characteristics. The very shape of the United States, for example, from the north western Washington border to the Florida peninsula, calls back to the conquests of the modern ideal. The Stars and the Stripes, the Capitol Building, the White House, even the commercial landscape—the *hypermodernist* aesthetic of globalization, with brand and corporate loyalty usurping the communion once provided by the church and nation—each of these are icons of the conquests of the modern ideal. In thinking on the exercise from the previous chapter, where we had subjected ourselves to an exploration of the United States Army Corps of Engineers' district maps, we became positively estranged from that residue.

Today, we stand within a vision of the **metamodern.** This vision is only possible after having left behind the sociologist's "man". We take our subject for economic reform as neither *a you,* nor *a me*; neither *a he,* nor *a she.* The subject of our prescriptions is the very condition for authenticity— that which we understand as a primordial discourse with nature. As the *subiectum* (as that which *establishes, builds,* *founds*, and *constructs* from *under, beneath,* and *at the foot of*), it is that which lies *below*, as the foundation for value creation. As such a foundation, discourse is pre-linguistic and pre-cognitive; discourse resists any appropriation into either language or knowledge. Therefore, we can only infer our subject through the very disclosure which comes forth out of the "radius" which is the πολις. This "coming forth" informs the orientation of our prescriptions. Our orientation is introverted back onto that which has come forth. This introversion promises novel discovery through elucidation. Modern man sought to conquer the moon. Let there be no doubt, then, that by tomorrow, this same "modern man" will have conquered Mars as well. And we let him go freely on his way to conquer even more territory after that. For us, we find our frontiers within the ruins left by this "man". And while the question of scale is undoubtedly of great importance to our own project at hand, for the time being, we must forfeit ourselves of any universal answers. The question of appropriate scale can only be answered by the author of any particular *there* and *then*. As such, our prescriptions *here* must be of a different type. We must limit ourselves to a localization of *the horizons of projection*. In order to do so, we must firstly acknowledge that the πολις has an epicenter, and from that center, truth extends towards a horizon. Everything that lies before that horizon is true; and everything that is beyond possesses no natural power. Once this much is acknowledged, and once we have firmly placed ourselves within one such center (as the epicenter of the πολις), then "localizing" refers to our commitment to that πολις—specifically, a commitment to look no further than what truth will allow. Anyone who makes this commitment will find themselves empowered by αληθευειν (as that "to truth"), which calls after action. As such, they will be unburdened by the need for any judgement over the truth. As we go forward towards our economic reform pre-scriptions, we must make this commitment so that anyone who finds themselves pulled towards the center of any one πολις can equally join others who are also being drawn to-wards the future to which the πολις projects.

Of course, pictures of a fractured United States are often painted with strokes of fear, anger, or exhaustion—from out of moments of forfeiture. These pictures are not only used to pander to the spirit of conservatism, but equally to those resonating with progressive narratives as well. The same can also be said for the British people's vote to exit the Eu-ropean Union. However, what is strikingly absent there is an ownership of such fracturing and exiting. Undoubted-ly, these movements attest to the spirit which pines for the conditions of truth and authenticity, even if so inexplicitly. However, without *governance as projection*, this spirit lacks a commitment to *society*. As long as this spirit suffers with-out this goal, the fracturing and exiting will persist as a re-gressive force and influence. Without this goal, these move-ments can neither sustain nor honor the atomic resonance which provoked them. And again, without it, we can expect that the search for truth will resume through alternative horizon-locating attempts—including especially violent measures, such as the isolation of "deplorable" worldviews where they can thus be eliminated.

Governance as projection seeks to remove the cleft which we have identified in the previous chapter—that between dis-course and truth. We expect that this removal will provide a venue and a forum for the disclosure of truth. Of course, in order to nurture authenticity within the reunion of dis-course and truth, we must not only provide for intimacy and listening, but also sympathy and understanding, trust and security for disclosure. No doubt, we sense hostility toward *the uncanny* and *the exotic* when we are placed under the pressing demands of "progress", "totality", and the "uni-verse". Therefore, truth and authenticity demand that we draw a definition, capturing a manifold for projection. Only with the definition of a project area can we expect an animation of that locus of value creation which we call authenticity. We understand that the very ideal of democracy demands such a novel definition.

Of course, the first expectation of any economic reform is the material welfare of the human animal. However, in starting firstly with *discourse* (as grounded in *projection*) as the subject of our economic reform prescriptions, we make a dramatic move—and one which we should expect, given the obstacles delivered over to us by way of the modern ideal. We are not particularly interested in satiating the human animal's hunger, his need for shelter, or anything like that, but rather in the spiritual satisfaction by way of such feeding and sheltering. We understand that the human animal is not merely to be fed at the trough, such that he could then go roll in the mud—as if spiritual satisfaction followed consequently from material satisfaction. If our economic reform prescriptions were not spiritual, then they would render themselves unnecessary. After all, there can be no doubt that capitalist economic systems have proven themselves to be materially satisfactory. Repeating the words of E.F. Schumacher (repeating Karl Marx before him), *"Conducting the entire economy on the basis of private greed has shown an extraordinary power to transform the world"*. Therefore, what is at stake in economic reform is *"not the standard of living but the quality of life"*. In other words, what is at stake is the soul. And yet, our starting position in metaphysical description allows us to go beyond the mere psychological and sociological diagnoses of Schumacher and Marx—

and this means that we can diagnose a more fundamental source of modern problems than either of these thinkers did. Furthermore, our solutions will have longer horizons. Inasmuch, our prescriptions provide us with the possibility of addressing Schumacher's greater insights,

> "A society ruled primarily by the idolatry of *enrichis-sez-vous*, which celebrates millionaires as its culture heroes, can gain nothing from socialisation that could not also be gained without it...If the purpose of nationalisation is primarily to achieve faster economic growth, higher efficiency, better planning, and so forth, there is bound to be disappointment."

> "Socialists should insist on using the nationalised industries not simply to out-capitalise the capitalists—an attempt in which they may or may not succeed but to evolve a more democratic and dignified system of industrial administration, a more humane employment of machinery, and a more intelligent utilisation of the fruits of human ingenuity and effort. If they can do that, they have the future in their hands. If they cannot, they have nothing to offer that is worthy of the sweat of free-born men."

A *spiritual* economic reform—one which provides for a more *"democratic and dignified system of industrial administration"*—this is the aim of our economic reform. We follow Schumacher's *Small is Beautiful*, fifty years behind.

With all of this now clearly stated, let us explicitly formulate those prescriptions which are available to us in the liminality of our today. Throughout the numbered list which follows, let us keep in mind that we are not prepared to present a static state utopia, such that we can then strategize towards that utopia. The modern ideal repels us. We begin within our standing position, *here* and *now*—from out of our inheritance. As such, our prescriptions must be delivered from the position of the authority to enact them. In the United States, in Europe, as well as in Russia we find both federal/confederal and unitary state models. No doubt, we should expect prescriptions to look differently when examined within each of these models. Therefore, we take as our example that which has remained closest to us since the last chapter. We limit ourselves to the federal/state model. Our prescriptions, therefore, will be delivered from this level of administration, presented as a platform for **a regionalization of governance** by way of *governance as projection* **civil works programs**. We can expect confederal and unitary state governing structures to be able to adopt this plan, with only slight modifications.

1. **Infrastructure.** What is required, firstly, is an infrastructure for enabling regional programs. We have already considered one possibility. Within the United States, the Corps of Engineers offers an infrastructure for flexing federal defense resources. What should be noted, in this case, is that flexing resources would not be tantamount to defunding defense programs outright. Yet, our platform does anticipate a deanimation of foreign interventionist policy. And this is, after all, consistent with the establishment of the Corps of Engineers, which traces its history back to 1802. That year was notable for being the date when Thomas Jefferson signed the Military Peace Establishment Act, thereby alleviating the need to employ expert engineers to foreign countries. Flexible resource allocation was of utmost importance in the establishment of the division. What is more?—by sharing military and civil works infrastructure, we also expect to address the

estrangement between these two spheres of commerce and among people who share a neighborhood, a family, and even between those who live within the same household.

2. **Financing.** We expect both operations and material procurement to be financed through productivity returns on state capital investments. We also expect accounting to be measured in terms of capital. In other words, our civil works programs must prove themselves financially. This is said explicitly in order to acknowledge concerns which follow from public-owned infrastructure—namely, concerns about inefficiency, waste, and the threat of corruption. Because we understand civil works programs as a mechanism of economic democracy, financial proofs and statements must be transparent to all stakeholders, including the recipients of the products of such programs. After all, only by ensuring this transparency can we be sure to uphold the ideal of democracy. Plus, by reuniting governmental administrative economy (including military operations) with civil economy, we can then also expect to achieve that aforementioned transparency. Despite this bid for state capital investment, we also understand that the total financing of our programs is pluralistic. We must take account of current tax revenue, for instance. However, let us also say that, in reverting the federal budget towards regional civic works programs, we also expect that programs could be sold-in at current tax rates. This is said in order to ensure that both the family and business sectors of commerce are not disrupted at the inception of any civil works program. Of course, with such a financing plan, it may sound to some as though we wish to "run the government like a business". And we must admit, this is partially true. Though, only partial-

ly. However, in order to understand this qualification, we must consider these programs within the rubric of value measurement.

3. **Value Measurement.** Firstly, we identify two channels for value measurement: a) the electoral process, and b) market economy. In the electoral process, value is measured by vote, and in market economy, likewise by sale. Up to this point, the development of this opuscule has not provided for an explicit phenomenological account of market economics. However, let us quickly do so now, for we have already prepared ourselves. Preliminarily, we must admit that market mechanisms do provide conditions necessary for authenticity. No doubt, the spirit for mercantilism is characterized by inspiration, lust, and a desire for engagement. What is more?—there seems to be no other economic narrative which can compete with the engagement of private entrepreneurship. Yet, as we have made clear, the horizons established through the market have not come to wholly satisfy our "long horizons". Alternatively, democratic election preserves projection towards *the good* and *the just—it preserves value.* Therefore, by way of the democratic election of both public officers and program projection we seek a hybrid of both long and short horizons within market economy. Our infrastructure must also encourage private entrepreneurs to propose civil works programs, and those entrepreneurs must be encouraged to create their own roles within the operation of the proposed programs, if they desire a role.

4. **Electoral Process.** Of primary importance to upholding the democratic ideal is the electoral process surrounding proposed programs. Our platform for *governance as projection* must provide for the *election of unique projects.* Bundling projects must be considered an exception—and

only when one project is financially dependent on another. There can be no "moral bundle". Therefore, our platform requires the establishment of an infrastructure for the creation of political parties with *project-based affiliations*. Such a transformation of party politics, from value-based identity-subject affiliations (progressives/conservatives, liberals/nationalists, democrats/republicans) to project-based affiliations, helps to secure a prefigurative approach to political activity.

5. **Recruitment and Remuneration.** Recruitment into positions below the electoral (that is, below *the proposal* and *strategic* functions) will follow existing open job market models. This includes both *managerial* and *operational* functions. Recruitment officers will offer attractive, market-competitive salaries and benefits.

Now, for some concluding remarks. The above five enumerated points are not exhaustive, and there is much room for interpretation. Of course, this is also intentional. However, our prescriptions must, therefore, also include guidance for interpretation. No doubt, that guidance can be found between the lines of text throughout the previous twelve chapters of this opuscule. Yet, there is one principal object which should be kept in the front and center of our mind's eye. It is worth repeating the name of that object once again—αληθευειν. Of course, securing conditions for αληθευειν is not something which could simply be accomplished through any one regional program alone. Securing αληθευειν will mean securing the processes of value measurement from interpretation as either a form of or platform for epistemological comportment (whether that measurement be through the electoral process, or by way of market indicators). We trust that this is possible, despite the fact that, for example, *greed* and *selfishness* are psychological diagnoses which often appear to successfully diagnose the motivations behind these processes today. Unfortunately, we cannot argue for any exact mechanisms by which to secure the conditions needed for $\alpha\lambda\eta\theta\varepsilon\upsilon\varepsilon\iota\nu$ here in this opuscule; this is on account that we have directed our proposal towards the federal level. Inasmuch, such mechanisms fall outside the scope of this work. Perhaps those mechanisms would make good content for a sequel to *How to Nurture Truth and Authenticity*. In any case, the best we can do here is to show that the possibility of protecting democratic election and market economy from such an interpretation does in fact exist. Let us now take the electoral process as our example. Consider the often-argued claim that exercising one's vote is an exercise of power—or that exercising the vote, in itself, is a thrust of one's own voice and an extension of one's own brute muscle. According to this reasoning, it appears as if the electoral process is the tool which we have adopted for the management of social power and, therefore, that the electoral process only animates the absolutism of the social power paradigm. Of course, regarding this "objection", we should be honest with ourselves. Our civil works programs are not an attempt to "overcome" the social power paradigm. This would, no doubt, be quite naïve. And, as we have made clear throughout our development, we are not here suggesting that the human animal might one day eradicate greed or selfishness absolutely. Instead, our attempts here aim at something much more dramatic. Our civil works programs are an attempt to create conditions in which psychological descriptions such as *greed* and *selfishness* lose their significance. We are interested in creating conditions in which it would do no one any good to diagnose these types of deviations. For sure, these descriptions, "greed" and "selfishness", belong to our form of life today. No one in their right mind would deny that. Yet, once standing in a position altogether besides the subjectivist paradigm and the subjectivist way of reasoning, and once standing in a position altogether beside the experience of social power, these diagnoses lose their significance. Consider how the exercising of one's voting privilege is not necessarily tantamount to an act of self-ishness or greed. We only need to remember that the vote is a mere object of measurement for what has already been secured, long before any ballot has reached the hand. Voting is not a thrust of command itself. Rather, it is a tool for measurement. We must likewise forgo that nagging thought which tells us that election is only possible following a series of persuasion campaigns. We are confident that securing the conditions for αληθεύειν is possible. After all, it is logically sound, at least. Therefore, it exists as a reality for us already in the *here* and *now* of today.

Of course, as with any nationalization platform, our proposal might also provoke suspicion regarding our motivations and intentions. And while we have expressed our dissatisfaction with the disclosure of truth as our motivation, we should still ask ourselves, in all honesty, *is our dissatisfaction perhaps a mere excuse?* We pose this question in all sincerity, and we do so not merely to ward off or to preemptively answer any potential challengers. We also ask this question in order to genuinely understand our own atomic motivations. After all, might it be more honest of us to say that our platform for *governance as projection* and civil works programs are a mere bid to preserve *the nation*, especially following the threat of dissolution in our globalizing economy?—a dissolution signalled by the success of crypto-currency or other nation-free currencies, among other nation-threatening indicators. Perhaps truth and authenticity are mere battle cries? Let us honestly answer ourselves regarding this question.

Looking back throughout the past twelve chapters, in an attempt to reflect upon this question, let us answer ourselves in this way: for those of us who understand the failure of the democratic institution of independent news media, and for those of us who understand the need for genuine authenticity in spite of the demand for unprecedented unity presented through today's social activism, and for those of us who are pulled towards actions to resolve modernization's alienation, rootlessness, estrangement, and apathy, we proceed *together*. We understand ourselves as genuinely motivated by a dissatisfactory commitment to truth and authenticity within today's interpersonal commerce. However, for those who discover within themselves motivations altogether besides this dissatisfaction, and who are perhaps, after all, "evil" national socialists who might encourage a fascist political economy in which the democratic institutions, education, news media, and market are each subjected to coercion from an elected party—for those of you, we must leave you behind. We do not stand with you. Then, for those challengers who remain suspicious of our motivations, who insist that our dissatisfaction with truth is a mere excuse and that our dissatisfaction merely serves to obscure some underlying "evil", let us make this much clearer: nurturing truth and authenticity by way of *governance as projection* is not tantamount to the preservation of the historical ethos of any country, despite our appeals to the political canvases of the United States, Europe, and Russia throughout this development. This opuscule has remained, from its inception, an economic reform proposal. And while it seems evident that many national ethoses have been sacrificed through liberal economic policy and the subsequent spread of globalization, we cannot use a schematic of ethos to pursue society. Let this much be clear—our prescriptions would be unbelievably naïve if we simply assumed the role of the anthropologist to prescribe a return to the American, Brittan, or Russian ethnos. No doubt, the economy in which the American ethos originated belongs to yesterday. Therefore, that ethos is impossible to reach *here* and *now*. Of course, the idolization of any historical ethos may help guide activity towards the future—we admit this. And yet, that future is something which must be written in those future moments. And with every new story, let there be a new ethos, respectively. At the same time, this does not neutralize, or in any way negate, our spirit for conservation. Our conservatism champions authenticity, and it does so in order to secure *the good, the beautiful,* and *the just* from subordination to the demands of material-technological progress and an algorithmic governance—those forms of governance in which truth is no longer a matter in the life of the human animal. Our prescriptions embody a progressive-conservative spirit. This spirit describes the behavior which acts in accordance with the promise of a future in which authenticity is liberated, such that the material substrate of the human animal is in service to authenticity. In fact, we understand that any material infrastructure can only be built upon that which is already in service to authenticity.

Of course, having said this, and when standing within a position which compels us to prioritize equal opportunity, our prescriptions might appear to be "missing the mark". Perhaps those who champion *Medical for All* might feel as though our proposal is half-assed. However, we understand that the material welfare of the human animal (and the material welfare of the earth's ecosystems in general) can only be built upon the conditions which allow for its sustainability. We understand those conditions as intimacy and listening, sympathy and understanding, trust and security for disclosure. Here we are referring to conditions which can only be felt in the moment, and measured through election. But once felt, these conditions proceed consequently into public welfare infrastructure and ecologically sustainable solutions. Inasmuch, we understand that any prescriptions for furthering public infrastructure by way of a nationalization of industry will be premature unless they are built upon the prescription of this proposal. Therefore, for those with such concerns, our prescriptions should be considered *strategic.*

The vision which we stand within calls after those who are humbled before it—those who understand its promises. This vision of a metamodern economic reform calls after those who can embody those promises, those who have the capacity for such embodiment, those who understand that this vision promises civic engagement towards the goal of *society.* We only hope that in this moment of our journey— the one towards liberation—we stand beside economic reformers who understand the promises of this vision, those who can embody those promises, that we ourselves may be those economic reformers.

Closing Exercise with Three Pictures

The futurism of yesterday had its own aesthetic. We recall the kinds of illustrations produced by hands possessed and enthralled by the modern ideal—exaggerated New York City art deco skylines, fantastic winged flying machines, the colonization of the moon, and so on. Yet, before this ideal could reach its pinnacle, it had already attracted the attention of detractors. The testimonies of these detractors are recorded into the postmodernist works of the last one hundred years. The suffering of these creators is evident in the alienation and rootlessness of industrial laboring; the estrangement and revenge of the post-colonial narratives; and the apathy, the cynicism and sarcasm, towards the giantism of modernization. While it is impossible to determine whether we have reached the peak of that suffering or not, or if more profound suffering still awaits us, we can still be confident that alternatives have already announced themselves by now—even if those alternatives only have the right to a visionary character. Insofar as this opuscule announces such an alternative, it has a fundamental right to such a vision. Undoubtedly, this opuscule has been built upon the ruins of industrialization, post-colonialism, and nihilism. But the gutters of that ruin are fertile flowerbeds.

While this opuscule can predict neither the future economy nor the functions to which truth will come to serve in that future economy, you can still do yourself one favor, already now; you can leave yourselves with one final exercise which may produce the proof of such a vision, if you are predisposed with the ability to consider such proof. After all, the proof which we are after here is illogical—yet, this must be admitted without shame. Proposals such as the one presented here can only be proven by means of the unquantifiable, the unmeasurable. They must show the way towards *the good, the beautiful,* and *the just.* Such proofs can only be described aesthetically.

Therefore, let us exercise that which has been teased since the very first pages of this opuscule—a subjection to a "safe space". Only in such a space can we encounter the aesthetic proof of our prescriptions. Of course, we understand that such a space is not opened in the abyss of thought, but in the laboring with that which shows itself, as it is, of itself. Your exercise *here* is then twofold. Allow yourself to be dominated by and dwell within this time. No doubt, you have felt the demand for such dwelling—a demand which comes from neither *me* the author, nor *you* the reader, but by the very commitment to truth and authenticity which adheres *now*. Despite the thirteen chapters that are now left behind you, with only one more to go, you are, in a way, still only one-third complete at this junction.

When you submit yourself to the imagery linked here by way of the forthcoming QR codes, ask yourself, *what type of economy is captured and represented in these pictures?* What objects motivate and maintain that economy? Are the objects named *soul* and *salvation* advantageous in any way? What of *free will*? Or *social power* or *economic competition*? Do these words explain the phenomenal experience in such

a way as to sustain and project the economy? Is there an understanding of *luck* which gives reason to the *wheeling and
dealing*? What of *fate*? What are the most effective *rulers*
used to measure the world? Is *society* one such ruler, as it
is ours today? Are offerings made to this god? Or has *harmony* rendered it satisfied? Can *truth* and *authenticity* guide
the economy through the labor of artistic creation? Or will
these objects also have become obsolete—perhaps they will
be replaced by algorithms?

Ask yourself, how is the material infrastructure maintained?
Would *ownership* be an accurate description, or would *us-
ership* be more appropriate? If the economy is pluralistic,
we can then ask, what shares are private when compared
to those that are public? Do any commons exist?—for example, facilities for medical treatment or for public education. Perhaps neither exist. It is possible to imagine another
form of education, after all. And how are the institutions
financed?—through taxation, or some other arrangement?

Ask yourself, how do you imagine value to be measured?
Through an electoral process? Through the market? And
how is the accounting done? By way of capital? Is there a
citizen's currency or other such allowance that is exempt
from exploitation? What are the roles and responsibilities
invested into each agent within the process of value measurement? Do you imagine a flat or a hierarchical society,
for example? Is there an aristocracy? A trend culture with
early and late adopters? What about the horizons of this
economy? City, region, or world governance? Will any of
these geographical definitions even have meaning? And
what about projection? How far does the economy project
into the future? Days, months, decades, or millennia? It is
reasonable to consider another form of life.

Perhaps in organizing your answers, you discover two categories: a best-case and worst-case scenario. In that moment, you can ask whether the prescriptions detailed within this opuscule project towards one or the other; in that moment, the proof will present itself over to you. In order to complete this exercise, open the camera on your smart device; point your device at the QR code. Then, wait for the camera to recognize and scan the code. Finally, click the banner or notification when it appears on your screen; the artwork will load automatically.

Matt Betteker
Concept Artist, USA/Denmark
Imaginary View of Grand Circus Park, circa 2189
2021, Digital

Matt Betteker
Concept Artist, USA/Denmark
View of Saint Peter's Cathedral from Orchard-South
2021, Digital

Matt Betteker
Concept Artist, USA/Denmark
Batteries at Bonnieville Farms with Visible Helixes
2021, Digital

>>> Objections to
the Proposal

Throughout the last fourteen chapters, we have allowed ourselves the freedom to make some dramatic claims—ones which do us no favors in defending the concluding prescriptions. Firstly, and top of mind, is our open challenge to the guiding values of liberalism. A nationalization of the economy through *governance as projection*, as well as our prescriptions for civil works programs to be sure, celebrates the idea of a reunion between liberalism's church and its state. Secondly, and on a more experiential level, we have not done ourselves any favors either. Remember that we have gone as far as challenging the value of doubt itself—a disposition which is often touted as healthy by both scientists and Christians alike. Perhaps even more existentially dire, we seem to have championed a subjectivity which has historically given rise to concerns of solipsism, and along with it, the need for proving the existence of the external world. Even in recounting this rather short list, we might find ourselves unwilling to defend any of the concluding reform prescriptions. What is more?—even this small recapitulation does not exhaust every reason for rejecting the proposal already. Yet, at the same time, we should not be shy in the face of these objections, or in the face of any others either. After all, if we are committed to nurturing both truth and authenticity, then we must explore such objections. Only in traversing them can we come to know whether we are prepared to defend the prescriptions herein; or if that defense belongs to another; or to no one at all. Of course, throughout our development, we have also tried to answer any immediate challenges, whether for the sake of our own convictions or in order to answer others. Yet, we still owe it to ourselves to follow up our proposal with a more thorough exploration of the potential objections. The first half of this exploration will focus on the philosophical foundations of our economic reforms. The second half will focus on the economic reforms themselves. Despite the efforts pursued over the next few pages, we should, of course, still not consider every objection to be exhausted.

Now, in order to firstly interrogate the philosophical foundations, we must return to the definitional chapters of this opuscule—those which initiated our metaphysical architectonic. We began those chapters by adopting Ancient Greek vocabulary by way of Richard Rojcewicz and André Schuwer's translations of material from the lecture course *Parmenides and Heraclitus*, prepared by Martin Heidegger. Then, by way of a deviation from the original lecture course material, we later pursued a more original set of vocabulary. By way of those aforementioned deviations, we arrived at a principal metaphysical claim—that the housing of αληθευειν in the economy of the πολις is a bias in the Western tradition, which, throughout modernization, has found many homes. In its widest sense, πολις defines the economy of mankind, of the human animal, "humanity". In order to shed such bias, we took up a phenomenological commitment as a virtue. This was done in order to preserve the "objective" domain and to recover truth from the relativism apparent in both anthropology and sociology. In preserving the "objective" domain—or rather *nature*, as that which *shows itself, as it is, of itself*—we also recovered ομοιωσις ("the disclosive correspondence expressing the unconcealed"). In recovering ομοιωσις, we were able to champion a truth not limited to the spoken or written word, or to any other phenomena originating from the human body. Instead, we positioned ourselves for accepting a disclosure of truth from phenomena altogether besides this type of animal. Αληθευειν (that "to truth" which is presenced in λογος) is unlike Aristotle's σοφος (*sofos*), τεχνιτης (*technitis*), or φρονιμος (*fronimos*)—those ways of human being. Rather, αληθευειν is the comportment of the world wholly.

However, and despite the promise of returning truth back to nature, we can also assume a twofold objection—one which is inherent to this very return. We ask, *is not the general character of our phenomenological commitment arrogance?* After all, if nature *"shows itself, as it is, of itself"*, then we can also do away with any need for doubt or skepticism—dispositions which are recognized as indications of epistemic humility. And neither do we default to *standardization as a ruler* by which to measure nature—that which is the foundation of positivism, the philosophy of all sciences. Our philosophy even seems to stand in opposition to the oft-mentioned Socratic Paradox, *ipse se nihil scire id unum sciat* ("I neither know, nor think that I know"), often colloquially phrased in Modern English as "all that I know is that I know nothing". And yet, our understanding of nature (as something which *"shows itself, as it is, of itself"*) seems to be a complete reversal of such humility. The truth of the world *"as it is"* means that *if some thing could be known, then that thing would be known*. Perhaps our reversal could instead be phrased as, *all that I know is everything that can be known.* Therefore, we are led to the objection, *is arrogance not the general character of our phenomenological commitment?* And on account of such arrogance, does our commitment not promote the brash bestiality often proscribed to Friedrich Nietzsche? Are we not morally obligated to reject such a phenomenological commitment? Yet, before we can answer this, we already come to the second objection which follows consequently from the first. Insofar as $αληθευειν$ is the comportment of the world wholly, human animals together with non-human animals and machines all collapse onto each other. Such a "collapse" provides for an animation of the ecological. However, our phenomenological commitment is not so much a bid for pantheism, such that food and chairs (or feminism and liberty, for that matter) are invested with the soul of the earth. Our commitment makes a bid for something much more frightening. While the ecological is elevated, the anthropological is also, at the same time, *de-animated.* We have **removed the soul from the human animal.** While we take this objection seriously, let us now consider it without the need for the word *soul,* or other such related terms. Such language dramatizes the situation on account of its occult characteristics and connotations.

In the initial chapters of this opuscule, we had called on the services of a useful fantasy. We imagined an organism which, by way of its commerce within its environment, created definitions in that environment, such that those definitions allowed for a more articulated commerce with its environment. Whether the organism of our consideration is some fantastical primordial ooze or simply a human baby, we can imagine the process of articulation—of drawing definitions in the sensual experience—such that the organism could have in its possession not only food and liberty, but also any particular *you* or *me*. That is to say, through articulation, we come to objectify objects—or, to use more scientific language, "cognitive representations". However, such a qualification of *objectified objects* over *cognitive representations* would, no doubt, offend any particular friend, colleague, or lover who we profess to be a mere "object" of our own needs—that is to say, that their constitution is what it is as founded on *my own personal commerce*. Or, in other words, what they are is not some substantial object (like a material body or a soul, for example), but are rather simply a value within my own life pursuits. Surely such an admittance would disgust anyone still harboring that feminist mantra of the late second millennium, that which insisted, "don't treat me like an object!" Here, and certainly now if never before, we must admit that defending this opuscule seems very undesirable. However, let us stop to reflect for just a moment.

Let us set aside some time for dwelling in our disgust. And why not? After all, we might be able to use such disgust to our advantage. By dwelling in such disgust, let us lower the shields which we had once raised in order to protect our phenomenological commitment. Let the arrows be launched! Because, if we are truly honest with ourselves, we are not yet through with our objections. To our twofold objection, let us now proceed to a third.

We have already qualified αληθευειν as a motionless action, as ομοιωσις. Αληθευειν is an adherence which provokes not mere cognitive thinking, but a more primordial *actio as reckoning*. And only on account of this reckoning can any subsequent mechanical action occur. In our vocabulary, αληθευειν calls after action which lags behind. That is to say, αληθευειν must be a more primordial movement than *willing*. Inasmuch, we must confirm that which was merely

teased back in chapter eleven, but was also left unacknowledged as an explicit objection. In order to uphold our phenomenological commitment, we must sacrifice that object
held for so long as something virtuous among those invested with the spirit for liberation—namely, *free will*. And this
subservience of one's own will to αληθευειν demands yet
another admission. With such a subservience of the will, we
must also surrender ourselves to fate. With such an admission, what we have now, by way of explicating a third objection, is a fourth. We are now in possession of a fourfold objection on account of our phenomenological commitment,

> Firstly, an arrogance tantamount to a reversal of the
> Socratic Paradox.

> Secondly, an objectification of our friends, family,
> and colleagues.

> Thirdly, a loss of one's own will.

> And finally, a complete surrender to fate.

Upon being presented with this fourfold objection, we seem
to have gotten ourselves into quite a nasty predicament.
The fourfold consequences of our phenomenological commitment seem to present ideal conditions for a life full of
hazardous activities. But then again, so what? Should we
then just leave it at that? After more than two hundred pages exploring the conditions for the disclosure of truth and
authenticity? After all, not only has this exploration led to
an identification of *episteme*, which has expedited imperial economy in the modern world, but it has also rendered
truth subservient to power. Therefore, before you proceed
to raze your copy of *How to Nurture Truth and Authenticity* into a pillar of flames, we should admit that these four

objections are nothing new within the discipline of philoso-phy. Endless hours have been dedicated to interrogating the phenomenological commitment through different logical treatments—even if such a "commitment" and such an "in-terrogation" have been inexplicit. Of course, philosophical claims of the type which follow from our phenomenolog-ical commitment are beyond the proofs we expect in, for example, the sciences. So, despite the fact that logic has of-ten been used for refuting the claims which follow from our phenomenological commitment, a logical argument is of little consequence. Philosophical claims of this type can only be "proven" in the soul, so to speak—if their pres-ence pulls us towards action in the moment of the encoun-ter. Therefore, instead of appealing to logic, we should ask, *what activities does our phenomenological commitment en-courage?* And yet, we have answered this question with our prescriptions. Our answer is ***governance as projection.*** For those who understand the promise of such a governance, let us now take each of these four objections, one at a time, so that we may be equipped to defend our proposal.

Firstly, let us answer those who make an objection on ac-count of arrogance. As should be clear, when we say that *"the world shows itself, as it is, of itself"*, we are not thereby saying that everything *"as it is"* is known in an epistemolog-ical sense. When we profess that *"all that I know is every-thing that can be known"*, we do not profess a totality—this much should be clear. After all, we have been critical of a "uni-verse" throughout the entirety of the development of this opuscule. However, if we were to attempt to respond to this critique by taking up our challengers' epistemological language, then we would say that our reversal of the Socrat-ic Paradox is merely an expression of honesty about what *is* known—and we make no presumptions that anything else *could* be known. Our reversal of the Socratic Paradox is a testament to proximity and the multi-stable constitution of phenomena. Once that humility is understood, then it is, perversely, the Socratic Paradox which anticipates imperialism, totalitarianism, and arrogance by way of a claim that *something else can be known which is not known to me now.* Perhaps we could express such Socratic arrogance by way of a simple question: *what else do you want the world to be, other than what presents itself over to you in each moment?* We should be careful of asking too much of the world and being led towards imperialistic pursuits. This resolve allows us to progress straight into answering the second of our objections.

While it may seem inhumane to say that any friend, colleague, or lover is merely an "object", and that their constitution is what it is as founded on *my own personal commerce*, no one should take offense to this type of language. After all, no moral prescription of behavior is consequent here. Any moral behavior is already inscribed within the constitution of the object itself. Simply consider the modern conception of a human animal—treating one of them as a beast of burden is simply inappropriate to the object *human animal.* Consider further the following objects we call *time, Pythagorean theorem, sun, bread and butter*—each are inscribed with the most appropriate ways of operating with the phenomenon identified as those objects. Of course, what is ultimately in question here is not the language of *objects*, but the value which is placed on any particular object, such that the moral behavior follows consequently. Morality can be followed as *a set of rules.* Yet, the question of value—that is, judgement—can only be understood in relation to the ruler by which any object is measured. While we may describe any particular product of the δημιουργος as good, beautiful, or just, it is by way of a phenomenological commitment that αληθευειν comes to stand in place of judgement. No ruler can be asked for with such a commitment—unless one wants to venture the very question regarding our form of life (and thereby present new rulers). So, if this language of objects encourages any morality whatsoever, then it is only to advance what is already becoming apparent; any value hierarchy between human animals, non-human animals, and machinery is becoming progressively less distinct.

What, then, of our third objection, namely, that regarding free will? Are we resigned into forfeiting this faculty, thereby depowering the epistemologist's individual-subject? On this point, what is demanded of the phenomenological commitment is, in all honesty, quite harsh. While this opuscule has been motivated by the spirit of romanticism, it has also been written *for* the romantic spirit. We must be passionate enough to forfeit free will to passion. This "must" is not merely a matter of *mustering* enough passion to be able to do so. Here, we are not asking for a *willing* in order to overcome the concept of "will". Such an ability to forfeit the will is either present, or it is not. If it is not, then we must say "yes", we are not prepared for the haphazardness which the fourfold objection anticipates—and then, in this case, neither are we prepared for nurturing the disclosure of truth. At the same time, we are not here to tout our own masterful disposition. We do not stand above those who lack the necessary maturity needed for nurturing both truth and authenticity. Only, we recognize that nurturing truth and authenticity itself demands its own conditions. Some of these conditions have already been explored in chapter eleven.

Of course, there is still the question of who *we* are?—that *we* referenced throughout this opuscule—the owner of *our* proposal. Throughout our development, the need for such a definition was lacking. But, just as the question presents itself now, at the same time, it also seems to resolve. The *we* of the liminal *here* and *now* does not indicate a *you* or a *me*— as in, for example, the relationship *author* to *reader*. The *we* could equally be expressed as *I, the one who resonates* with the words herein—whether that be *me* the author, *you* the reader, or neither of us. Yet, this ambiguity also gives us an explanation as to why the *we* has not been explicitly identified. The object which the *we is* referring to can only be identified outside the pages of this opuscule. At the same time, such an identification cannot be made by simply presenting ourselves as the object *I*. Even if such a presentation would be made—whether from the mouth of any human animal, a non-human animal, or a machine—the *I*, as that *we*, would still not have been identified. The *we*, as *the one who resonates* with the words herein, cannot be shown by such presentations. This *we* either presents itself, or it does not. No proof can be given for it. This is an expression of humility regarding the limits of what can be known to us, and that we take for granted an *us*, and, furthermore, that we do so without any demand for empirical proof.

At this point, we must say "so long" to the moral objections towards our phenomenological commitment on account of either an epistemological arrogance, or an objectification of human animals; a loss of personal will, or a surrendering of our future to the hands of fate. We must leave these objections aside. But, in doing so, we can assume that we have forestalled any of the critics who may want to "one up" our proposal on such an account.

Now, while the spirit of romanticism has helped to motivate the creation of this work, we must nevertheless also acknowledge a parallel future narrative which can be found arising from out of the ruins of liberalism. Given the per-vasiveness of episteme today, we should not be surprised by the persistence of this narrative. This is the story of surveillance technology—the story which is envisioned in cyberpunk dystopias and other fantasies which tease the complete and utter loss of liberation for authenticity. And while we admit that this story is quite fantastical, it is only because we understand its reality, today, that it can provoke our reckoning. We do live with that future vision, *here* and *now*. No doubt, communist China often serves as the object for the associated fears. Cyberpunk futurism has been tied up with Asian cultural themes. However, in acknowledging this future reality, we must also admit that our two future "alternatives" are not diametrically opposed. Standing here, in this *"time between worlds"*, we must admit that even our own economic prescriptions might come to perversely serve in the making of this future. Therefore, we can use these visions of dystopian cyberpunk surveillance states to draw out an objection to our material reform prescriptions. Only in traversing this objection can we come to know whether or not we are prepared for defending the prescriptions as a whole.

We are now reflecting on our platform for a **regionalization of governance** by way of **civil works programs**. To do so, we return to our financial expectations. Both the operations and material procurements of our civil works programs are to be financed through productivity returns on state capital investments. That is, accounting will treat of measured state capital within a market economy. However, here we must admit to a haunting suspicion. Within Marxist literature, state capitalism has been treated as an inceptual-stage condition towards a planned economy, as well as a type of social ownership over the means of production. Let us recall that for Vladimir Lenin, "[In state capitalism] *the capitalist relationship isn't abolished; it is rather pushed to the extreme. But at this extreme it is transformed into its opposite. State ownership of the productive forces is not the solution of the* [class] *conflict, but it contains within itself the formal means, the key to the solution*".

Therefore, we must ask, *do we understand as Lenin?* Are we projecting ourselves towards a planned economy and a social ownership over the means of production by way of our civil works programs? After all, how are *regional projects* supposed to compete alongside *global agents* in an open market? If regional projects are to remain competitive, then we should expect accompanying tariffs. And furthermore, when faced with financially failing projects, protectionist policy will follow. Project officers will, no doubt, seek self-preservation. Personal career and family livelihoods will be at risk. And by way of internal lobbying, it is hard to imagine any other outcome than a state domination of the market. Therefore, in localizing the horizons of our projections, are we not doomed for regional inbreeding? And can we honestly defend our prescriptions when fears of protectionism and subsequent isolationism loom—least of all to ourselves? No doubt, these are dire questions indeed. And yet, we have not come to the end of our reasoning. After all, if our regional projects are to be truly market competitive, then they require the pursuit of cutting-edge technology. Presented with prospects of a state-regulated economy on top of a state-owned technology industry, we tease our fears of dystopian cyberpunk surveillance states. At this point, we may want to ask, *how are our future visions any different from what will be encouraged through the "utilitarian state" of liberalism?*—that *governance as law* which is subjected to coercion from market interests and is currently driven by the financial and big tech industries? What power or security is granted to the people to counter either industrial machine?

While thinking about such dire considerations, we should remember that the early Marxists touted the proletariat uprising and communist revolution as a culmination of a material dialectic. With such an understanding, Marxists pursued a static state economy, a system which was believed would solve the "boom and bust" of privately-owned uncoordinated production. However, in the practice of the Soviets, barometers for value measurement were underutilized; and, without either a healthy electoral process or market indicators for determining value, the human soul is equally static. The soul of the Russian had succumbed to the reasoning of a single party and its monological industrialization towards a long-prophesied future. However, and while we might have initial concerns that our own platform leads us towards this same type of static state in the future, we can be assured that we have already secured ourselves against it.

Let us remind ourselves that the human animal and its technological future are also natural. Neither modernization nor the material development of technology are a cosmic force opposed to "man". Nature is that which shows itself, as it is, of itself "yes"—but, at the same time, adherence to that appearance provokes a primordial reckoning—this primordial reckoning calls after mechanical action. Any mechanical action only makes actual what was already reckoned in the presencing moment of authenticity. And so, just as tectonic shifting has produced beautiful mountain visages, the mechanical actions of technology are to be experienced as a natural pleasure as well. What is required then for quelling fears of dystopian cyberpunk surveillance states are exactly what the Soviets had neglected—barometers for value measurement. And yet, barometers for value measurement, and in particular the measurement provided by democratic election, are precisely what free market agents lack. Elon Musk. Bill Gates. The contributors to the World Economic Forum—those who champion a "Great Reset". While these agents are subjected to market demands, they are also removed from the value measurement provided by the electoral process—that which measures *the good* and *the just* and projects us towards long horizons. Let us make our case by way of example. How could a conquest of Mars or commercial travel to space mean anything to us today except as an expression of decadence? Of course, a retort may be given that it is because pursuits to domesticate space such as these can drive technological advancement—and the resulting technology produced as a by-product of that advancement might prove itself to be applicable towards other human efforts (perhaps a domestication of space replaces military defense in this regard). Yet, let us ask ourselves: in all honesty, *are we so amused by technological advancements?* If we allow ourselves a bit of introspection, is it not rather the case that we celebrate the decadence of the free market agents as a justification—and that what is at issue is not material welfare and/or technological advancement, but is instead something actually quite spiritual? Today, we read testimony which proves the spiritual leadership provided by free market agents. Yet, their spiritual leadership is not on account of the quality of their personal character, or any other product which they offer. Rather, we follow their "teachings" on account of the influence which their decisions hold over our own personal investment in the stock market. The reward of following their "teachings" is that we too can be financially successful. Of course, the stock market could provide a model for coordinating a "collective wealth of the people" counter to that of state economics. And this would be fine if the only satisfaction we sought was a kind of material self-satisfaction. Because, if we are truly honest with ourselves, in this possible future, without accompanying electoral processes, any stock holder's life is then reduced to something even less than a slave's. At least the slave is free to create a ressentiment value in the face of his master, while the stockholder would not be. So, while it may seem perverse, electoral *governance as projection* by way of state infrastructure and its accompanying proximal civic engagement does secure a pluralistic and democratic economy in the future, today.

Of course, standing here at this very moment, it may appear as if market regulation is the only lever we can pull. And the only hope for democracy is protectionist policies. Yet, at the same time, we have not yet set any limitations to the procurement of raw materials or any other resourcing needs within our civil works programs. And neither have we defined the market to which any regionally engineered product or service is to reach. Our only "limitation" regards market measurement itself. This is solely because of its insufficiency in measuring value. By "limiting" the market, the electoral process can be animated. And for the time being, we cannot, in good conscience, do more. Yet, our allowance of resourcing, procurement, and market definition to persist interregionally only emphasizes our primary objective. Here, we are not interested in domesticating the human animal. Ours is not a platform to be maintained through violence, but instead through the election of that which is proximally within reach, and where the reach of the ballot is what determines the region, and where *the good, the beautiful,* and *the just* have revealed, in full clarity, a projection towards the future for that region.

Let us now make one final admittance before we end this brief exploration of potential objections. In prioritizing *the good, the beautiful, the just,* and *the true,* we are more or less aesthetically oriented. Yet, at the same time, we are not blind to the fact that any appearance of aesthetics in the realm of politics often produces discomfort. There has been an expectation that politics must be objective—that decisions taken by politicians are only done so on behalf of that statistically apprehended "public". This expectation holds that politicians are merely our servants, and when this expectation is not met, we are disappointed in them. Yet, at the same time, we also acknowledge that aesthetic value itself is not to blame, nor the fact that politicians are, after all, human. To believe that we could remove aesthetics from politics is a self-deception. Having acknowledged this, we must look elsewhere to diagnose the discomfort which results from the thought of aesthetically-driven politics. When we do, we find that it is a lack of tools for the creation and maintenance of aesthetic value within the public sphere which is to blame. Yet, for the sake of the soul of the earth, we must allow the public sphere, if it is to be a natural sphere, to be a source of aesthetic value. This does not mean that we are committing ourselves to the idea that politicians be celebrities and idols of value. We are here not suggesting a cult of personality. But it does mean that we, each of us, as politicians, must fulfil our nature as originators of value in the civic domain. In announcing aesthetics, we have not thereby made politics more difficult. Instead, we are liberated thanks to a better understanding of the tools which make operating with aesthetics possible in the first place.

>>> Annotated
Bibliography

Producing a bibliography comprising every publication which has influenced the creation of *How to Nurture Truth and Authenticity* must be an impossible task. Such a list of publications is not even known to me, the author of that opuscule. Yet, at the same time, I also understand that there is no need for such a comprehensive bibliography anyway. Despite this, I do understand that my reader may find interesting the publications which were studied during the execution of my work. I understand that such a list might help to place my reader in a frame of mind similar to my own, during that time. Therefore, this bibliography has been written for that purpose.

How to Nurture Truth and Authenticity was constructed in just over a year, between 2020 and the first months of 2021. Then, after discovering the *first economics* description and narrative nearer to the completion of earlier drafts, a revision was necessary. That revision spanned the summer months of 2021. Therefore, the below list of publications includes those which were studied during 2019, leading up to the conception of my work, along with the publications studied during its execution in 2020 and 2021. In order that this bibliography can serve its purpose, I have chosen to annotate the list. This, I hope, provides my reader with the answers which any bibliography could promise. The list is arranged in alphabetical order, using the author's last name.

William Blattner

Heidegger's Temporal Idealism. Cambridge University Press, 1999.

There is no hiding the influence which Martin Heidegger's early metaphysics have had on the opuscule. And, after all, I do understand Heidegger as the premier metaphysician to be contended with, and still so to this day. This I say, despite the amount of academic output which has been produced on account of his work, seemingly exhausting the potential novelty of its interpretation. However, if I thought academia could exhaust the value of Heidegger's works, then this would be to take those works as merely of intellectual interest. Yet, this is not the case. I understand that the value of Heidegger's early metaphysics could only be exhausted from within the political realm. While this is perhaps a quite strong claim, I feel prepared to defend it. Therefore, I see no reason to revert political theory to a time before Heidegger's metaphysics of *Being* and *Time* and his so-called "anthropological" exposition. From our vantage point, we can only go forward. This holds, despite the many attempts to recover epistemological metaphysics from Heidegger's mere *"philosophical anthropology"* (Edmund Husserl)—whether that recovery were to come in the form of Jean-Paul Sartre's *existentialism*, or Theodore Adorno's *negative dialectics*, or through the contemporary philosopher John Vervaeke's *transjectivity*. Heidegger's influence is apparent in any one of them; it seems that, even as epistemologists, we are indebted to Heidegger's metaphysics. I understand that this is the case, even if, in going forward, we also move away from that anthropological exposition and towards the cosmological. Not even Yuk Hui's *cosmopolitics* can exist without Heidegger's metaphysics. Therefore, we cannot disavow ourselves of either Heidegger or of his influence on us, even as cosmopoliticians.

Now, having said all of that, at the time of writing this bibliography, it seems to me that only William Blattner has offered a critique which puts Heidegger's fundamental ontology, as described in *Being and Time*, in jeopardy. However, as Blattner admits, even if Heidegger's project fails to ground *time* upon *originary time*, this has not destroyed the value of his project outright—and neither will this have destroyed Heidegger's position as the premier metaphysician from which contemporary metaphysicians and political theorists must proceed. It is on this account that I can say that Blattner's own successful critique has also furthered the discipline of metaphysics and political philosophy. After all, I understand Blattner's *Heidegger's Temporal Idealism* as the premier secondary literature on Heidegger's early metaphysics of value creation.

Daphne Büllesbach, *et al.*

Shifting Baselines of Europe: New Perspectives Beyond Neoliberalism and Nationalism. transcript Verlag, Bielefeld, 2017.

At the inception of my opuscule, I had no idea that I was going to produce a critique of liberal values, nor present prescriptions for economic reform which could rightfully fall under the banner of nationalism. At the inception of this project, I only knew the scale of governance was to be a central issue—and this, I knew, regarded both the governance conducted by way of public administrators and social justice activists. I understood that the scale of our discourse (as that which precedes these forms of governance) was the cause of much suffering. I knew that I needed to champion local canvases of governance. However, as my argument crystalized, and as my critique of liberal values became significant, *Shifting Baselines of Europe* offered me a contemporary critique of nationalism—a critique which I could extend to even the "Left-friendly" version of nationalism: *civic nationalism*. Now, because I would happily classify the prescription of the opuscule under the banner of democratic nationalism, I have attempted to address some of the concerns presented in *Shifting Baselines of Europe*. This is in order to preemptively answer any critics. Despite this, the most important content of *Shifting Baselines* to my own work were the interviews with activists from within the municipalist movement. This was, after all, the movement which led me to this publication.

Aleksandr Dugin

The Fourth Political Theory. Arktos Media, 2009. Trans. Mark Millerman.

Unfortunately, a suitable location for reflecting on the Russian political strategist Aleksandr Dugin did not present itself anywhere throughout my development. And, on that account, if for no other reason, this bibliography demanded to be written. After all, it could be argued that the opuscule, taking up Heidegger's early metaphysics of value creation as it does, could rightfully be classified as a work of Fourth Political Theory. And yet, as apparent as that may be, it is yet to be decided if that classification would be justified. In order to either accept or reject that classification, we have to first decide upon the relationship between Dugin as a political strategist, and his own theory. That is, we have to decide if Dugin has simply announced Heidegger's *da sein* as the subject of a new political theory, or if Dugin himself is also an activist of his Fourth Political Theory. While this may seem like a round-about concern regarding the classification of the opuscule as a work of Fourth Political Theory, there is good reason for it. After all, we should beware of the fact that if we accept this classification, then we might also, as a consequence, align ourselves with Aleksandr Dugin, the activist. Of course, coming to such a decision about the relationship between Dugin and his own theory may seem overly easy—we may want to say that Dugin, of course, is an activist of his own Fourth Political Theory. However, there is good reason for deciding otherwise.

Now, in considering the relationship between Dugin and his Fourth Political Theory, we must, at first, remember that Dugin has firmly placed himself within the position of *"the omniscient world observer"* of either sociology, and/or of scientific anthropology. As such, his *being* is as a scientist; we can be sure of this. Certainly, when he calls for his multiculturalism, he sits in that position. In doing so (that is, in accounting for the multiplicity of cultures), Dugin is committing himself to the idea that each culture has their own inherent truth—that is, to the idea that truth is relative. Specifically, he champions for *"the unique Russian truth."* Inasmuch, we can make quite a dramatic claim about Dugin himself. Insofar as liberal political activity is preoccupied with the security of individual or group beliefs by way of securing the rights of those individuals or groups, we can thus venture out to call Dugin an identity politics liberal. Of course, I do understand that this is most likely a shocking claim. Anyone championing for liberal economic policy, liberal immigration policy, or a mixing of the cultures and races in some capacity, would surely understand Dugin as an opponent. From those positions, and insofar as Dugin champions for something of a *separate but equal multiculturalism,* most opponents would understand him as an ethnonationalist. We might categorize these objections to Dugin as *the liberal critique,* or *the critique from the Left.* And yet, it is precisely because Dugin champions for rights so much (in his case, the right for minority cultures who are jeopardized by globalization to continue into the future) that the spirit of the Right can equally align with those provocateurs who name him *"the most dangerous thinker today".*

While Dugin has announced Heidegger's *da sein* as the subject of a new political theory, he is, from *a post-liberal position,* that *"omniscient world observer"* operating within epistemological metaphysics, which is also the foundation for the subject/object dichotomy, epistemological relativism, and the virtue of objectivity (as that which reckons with relativities). As a political strategist and political activist who equally reckons with relativism by way of objective reasoning, Dugin is, therefore, a progenitor of the epistemological paradigm. Heidegger's life's work can be understood as an attempt to progress further onwards from this paradigm. Any political strategy or political activity founded upon Heidegger's metaphysics will equally have progressed from epistemological political strategy and political activity. Therefore, decidedly and from a post-liberal position, Dugin does not present the political activity of a Fourth Political Theory activist. And, insofar as his activity does not present a foundation in Heidegger's metaphysics, his popularity stands as an obstruction for anyone whose activity does present that foundation. This, then, is quite an unfortunate state of affairs for political theory in general, to be sure.

Of course, outside of the question of Dugin's relationship to Fourth Political Theory, we can sympathize with the apparent intentions behind Dugin's *separate but equal multiculturalism*. Surely globalization demands critical attention "no"? It would be a shame if the world were to be consumed by American imperialism via market economics—that is to say, it would be a great loss if the world were consumed by *a commodity culture*. Without a doubt, the spirit of the Right is well-equipped for a critique of such imperialism and, similarly, such cultures also. Therefore, let us sympathize with those who champion for "*the unique Russian truth*", as Dugin does. But let us beware in doing so. Let us sympathize without taking up relativism into our own philosophical constitution.

No doubt, Heidegger's metaphysics, as expounded upon in *Being and Time*, do encourage the explication of a new political theory. The evidence for this is the explanatory power of those metaphysics, which have usurped those of the epistemological metaphysics of Enlightenment literature (and the political manifestation of those metaphysics, which we call *liberalism*). No doubt, a new political theory which takes Heidegger's *da sein* as its subject will have *a post-liberal character* about it; Dugin has correctly identified this. However, this post-liberal political theory could never be presented through the mere documentation of the many worldviews which the human animal has produced. Neither could it be presented through the management of those many worldviews. In the introduction to *Being and Time*,

Heidegger offers the same diagnosis by way of a psychological diagnosis of *da sein*,

> *"Da sein* has had its historicality so thoroughly *up-root by tradition* that it confines its interest to the multiformity of possible types, directions, and standpoints of philosophical activity in the most exotic and alien of cultures, and by this very interest it seeks to veil the fact that it has no ground of its own to stand on. Consequently, despite all its historiological interests and all its zeal for an interpretation which is philologically 'objective', *da sein* no longer understands the most elementary condition which would alone enable it to go back to the past in a positive manner and make it productively its own."

As I have argued throughout the opuscule, Heidegger's *"elementary condition"* begins with the phenomenological method and ends in economic reform. Therefore, more crystalline than a new political theory which takes *da sein* as its subject, would be a new political theory as one of value creation—that is, one which is beyond myth (Dugin) and is essentially economical in nature.

Now, what has been argued for here is also, admittedly, quite a shame. It is unfortunate that Dugin, as a political strategist, does not represent a political theory which takes Heidegger's *da sein* as its subject. Because, despite all of the critics, there is value in *a cult of personality*. And, of course, Dugin nearly fits the bill. His position within history, as the premier Russian philosopher at the time of the collapse of the USSR, makes him well suited for being that personality. But, of course, we should always be true to ourselves when looking for personalities to embody our values. If we honor those values, then we must place personality second; otherwise, we risk confounding the values with the personality. Therefore, for those of us standing with the hopes of something resembling a Fourth Political Theory—that is, a political theory which takes Heidegger's *da sein* as its subject —then we must let Dugin fall to critique. And we must do this, despite the possibility that, in Dugin's absence, we will be presented with a void instead.

Steven M. Feldman

The Problem of Critique: Triangulating Habermas, Derrida, and Gadamer Within Metamodernism. Contemp Polit Theory 4, 296–320 (2005).

If you allow me, for a moment, to step away from the list of publications which I studied during 2019, 2020, and 2021, then I am free to tell a bit of personal history preceding these years. This history is necessary for understanding the debt which I owe to Steven M. Feldman's *The Problem of Critique: Triangulating Habermas, Derrida, and Gadamer Within Metamodernism.*

In 2009, I returned to an intellectual life pursuit following an introduction to Friedrich Nietzsche's *Thus Spoke Zarathustra.* However, in 2017 and following the election of Donald Trump to the presidency of the United States, my interests turned from philosophy to political philosophy. It seemed to me that, following this election, the integrity of the democratic institutions had collapsed, and truth had come into the spotlight by way of the post-truth media frenzy. Furthermore, the individual had been sacrificed; the political climate had escalated to a state of giantism, such that *the personal* had been subsumed to tribes of social activists. At some point during that same year, I had also read a commentator naming Trump as the first "postmodern president". During the process of producing my first collection of writing about this so-called *postmodern condition*, I then discovered the metamodern narrative. Metamodernism's return to romanticism immediately resonated with me. Following this, I found myself possessed with the spirit of "the meta". However, it was not until I had encountered Feldman's *The Problem of Critique* that I was able to bring the metamodern narrative into alignment with my own. While that alignment with metamodernism also took on a critical form, I still understood the metamodern narrative as relevant for defining a politically useful history. This understanding still persists, up to this very moment. Additionally, it was firstly in Feldman's article that I had identified "the epistemological sociologist", a type which could be applied to later political activists—whether that be the social activist of wokism or the parody of this social activist, as evident in the gang weed Joker meme, *we live in a society*.

Today, from the vantage point of present time, we can characterize Feldman's metamodernists (namely, Habermas, Derrida, and Gadamer), and, along with them, the critical theorists of the same period, as harbingers of the third millennium's "armchair sociologist".

Emil Ejner Friis and Daniel Görtz

The Listening Society: A Metamodern Guide to Politics. Metamoderna ApS, 2017.

It was sometime in 2017, when an article posted to the Philosophy Matters Facebook page had first introduced me to the metamodern narrative. After reaching out to the authors of this article, *The Difference Between Post- and Meta-modernism* (also the authors of *The Listening Society*), Daniel Görtz invited me to join a forum with the purpose of discussing and organizing the metamodern political movement. Prior to my involvement in this movement, I had not spent much time with committed sociologists. Therefore, it should be no surprise then that during this time, I first discovered my discomfort with *the logic of society: sociologic*. And, as is quite obvious by now, I had constructed *How to Nurture Truth and Authenticity* with a purpose to challenge the application of this science to political theory and political activity. Yet, despite the popularity of this logic within the metamodern movement, I would not recount my time spent within this movement negatively. It was, after all, my discomfort with sociology which allowed the discipline of metaphysics (and, specifically, Heidegger's early metaphysics of value creation) to present itself in contrast. Eventually, it was an intolerance for the critical methods common among sociologists, those fueled by doubts and anxieties (alongside the explicitly acritical romanticism promised of metaphysics) which allowed *first economics* to announce itself. Today, from the position of *first economics* philosophy, the work of these Scandinavian metamodernists, including *The Listening Society* and the second book in the series, *The Nordic Ideology*, remain as mere objects for critical analysis, such that the discipline of metaphysics and *first economics* philosophy may be pronounced through the contrast. Of course, this is not to say that when standing within the discipline of sociology, the analyses of Friis and Görtz are incorrect. After all, they might very well produce good results. For my part, I have found their analyses to be quite elucidating, particularly the reflections on governance by "*negative emotion*" and shame culture (*The Nordic Ideology*). Yet, despite all of this, the discipline of sociology cannot provide for progress from out of modernity's imperialistic essence. This is evident in that the discipline is built upon episte-mology's individual-subject. This holds true even when that subject is modified into a sociological subject, such as the case with Gilles Deleuze's *"dividual"*. Of course, it is likely that Friis and Görtz would accept the imperialistic char-acterization of their prescriptions. After all, they make the seemingly perverse claim that *"more control equals more freedom"*. And yet, while their point has been made, this does not bode well for either truth or authenticity—or for anyone wishing to *listen* to anything other than their own thoughts, repeated in the mouth of another.

Michael Allen Gillespie

Heidegger's Aristotelian National Socialism. Political Theory Vol. 28, No. 2 (Apr., 2000), pp. 140-166. Sage Publications.

Characterizing *Heidegger, the statesman,* is a project which does not appear to be too uncommon among academic lit-erature. Perhaps it was Leo Strauss who had prepared for this. After all, he is most likely to be the one responsible for popularizing the question of Heidegger's commitment to *the political,* outright. However, and despite the avail-ability of the literature, it is the succinctness of Michael Allen Gillespie's *Heidegger's Aristotelian National Socialism* which proves itself to be quite useful in answering Heide-gger's relationship to politics. What becomes apparent through Gillespie's article is that a Straussian preoccupa-tion with *natural rights* (as it appears, for example, in his lecture course material on Friedrich Nietzsche's *Thus Spoke Zarathustra*) is exactly that which prevents an understanding of Heidegger's politics. However, once the priority of *rights* is abandoned altogether (and, along with it, the responsibility of a governance to secure those rights), then a fresh intellectual space opens up. In that space, novel forms of governance are allowed to fill the void. In order to understand exactly how far outside of rights Heidegger's thinking is situated, let us consider that ideal which rights are supposed to secure—namely, *freedom*. Let us do so by way of *Heidegger's Aristotelian National Socialism*, together with Gillespie,

> "Heidegger understands freedom in an essentially Greek fashion as the freedom of the people that arises from giving themselves their own laws (i.e., from constituting themselves as a people). Such freedom thus is not individual freedom. Indeed, it imposes new duties on individuals. The duties and social roles that fall to individuals will vary, but they will not be determined by theoretical or technical necessities. Social differences based on economic or technical distinctions will be swept away and replaced by the human distinctions that arise out of the needs of the people."

Following Gillespie's interpretation of Heidegger's conception of freedom, and his interpretation of Heidegger's projection for the future of National Socialism, the project to characterize something like *Heidegger, the statesman* appears to be ill-founded—of course, this is the case, insofar as we understand the modern state in a thoroughly liberal fashion (that is, as invested with the responsibility to secure rights for the sake of individual or group freedoms). Heidegger's freedom, you could say, is prior to the establishing of laws for the protection of rights, or of other such legislation. However, in the absence of any prioritization of liberalism's rights, and in looking towards a more foundational under-standing of governance (as Heidegger did), we can ask, *if not rights, then what exactly are we supposed to think when we think of governance*? For Heidegger, governance begins, firstly, in the relationship between the δημιουργος and the δημος.

Now, it should be said that Gillespie's interpretation of Heidegger's so-called "Aristotelian National Socialism" fol-lows from Heidegger's lecture course material from the win-ter semester of 1924–1925, at the University of Marburg—material which was later published under the title *Plato's Sophist*. This is evident in the succinct recapitulation of the preparatory interpretation of Aristotle's *Nicomachean Ethics* from that lecture course material. Gillespie's recapitulation provides for the force of his article. However, underlying his recapitulations is an attempted critique—and this cri-tique is evidently not intended for mere analysis, but rath-er, to be used as an attack on Heidegger's political project outright as it manifested through his rectorship at Freiburg University. In particular, Gillespie is critical of Heidegger's endorsement of the *führerprinzip*—that is, the principle that the leader is always right and that his words demand total obedience. We will proceed with a consideration of Heideg-ger's political project at Freiburg by way of Gillespie's article, then we shall consider Gillespie's critique,

> "[Heidegger] first attempted to reorganize the uni-versity according to the *führerprinzip* to refound it on the basis of a philosophical questioning of Be-ing. He sought to push individual disciplines and departments to consider fundamental questions. He also enthusiastically attempted to insert labor and military training exercises into the curriculum to counteract what he saw as the hyperintellectualism

of students and faculty. Finally, he organized science camps (retreats for selected members of the faculty and a few students) according to the *führerprinzip* to try to integrate the practical and theoretical sides of education."

For Heidegger, the *fühur* must have, as his way of being δημιουργος, not in the sense of a god-creator—which Heidegger designates as φυτουργος (*fytourgos*)—but as a craftsman who produces the ιδεα of the δημος. That is to say, the δημιουργος produces the outward appearance of the world within the commerce of the public usage of things and of communal life. If we understand democracy—that is, a rule by the people—not from the perspective of top-down government administration, but in the sense of communal economy, then Heidegger's endorsement of the *führerprinzip* is democratic. Remember that the production of the δημιουργος is, and can only ever be, a manifestation of ιδεα insofar as the δημιουργος is equally being as the δημος. That is to say, the ιδεα essentially belongs to *the people*. Therefore, the δημιουργος can only ever *merely* present the ιδεα through such production, being as one such instance of *the people*. Consequently, if the ιδεα is not of the δημος, then neither is the being of the producer as δημιουργος.

Gillespie's further evidence for the failure of Heidegger's phronetic political project is that "*in the aftermath of* [Heidegger's] *failure* [at Freiburg]", Heidegger turns from considerations on *death* to considerations on *Being*. And while this is true, what should not be shunted aside is that Gillespie delivers a historical reason, not a theoretical one. Of course, this bibliography is not an appropriate place to consider Heidegger's historical turn from death to Being. However, what must be apparent to anyone here, already, is that Heidegger's failure at Freiburg does not speak towards a failure of a theory of political economy founded upon proximal φρονησις; such a proof could only be found in the rejection of such a theory, *today*. Therefore, if Heidegger's failure can be said to have proven anything, then it is the less interesting failure of such a political economy within the canvas of National Socialist Germany. In other words, it is the case that Heidegger failed as a Nazi,

> "All of Heidegger's efforts failed. In part, this was because the [Nazi] party was suspicious of his intellectualism and his Jesuit and Jewish connections. A more important reason for his failure, however, was resistance from within the university and especially from the natural scientists who did not want their research programs derailed by philosophical questioning. The faculty as a whole was also bitterly opposed to required labor and military exercises. Faced with this failure and unwilling to compromise with either the party or the faculty, Heidegger resigned."

Now, already at the inception of his article, we find Gillespie preparing us for his conclusion, which is to show that *"Heidegger's vision of* φρονησις *(fronēsis,* "prudence, practical wisdom") *is fundamentally flawed"*—or rather, that Heidegger's theory of a political economy founded upon φρονησις is fundamentally flawed. To do so, Gillespie begins his interpretation following a particular reading of *Being and Time*—namely, that "φρονησις *is not present in all human beings. Indeed, for the most part, human beings are lost in their everyday concerns"*. While this understanding does follow from Heidegger's words, when using it to understand Heidegger's endorsement of the *führerprinzip*, it is ultimately inconsistent with the authentic/inauthentic nature of *da sein*, as Heidegger expounded upon it in *Being and Time*. The possibility of authentic and inauthentic moments is an essential characteristic of *da sein*, in each and every case. This would be true for the *führer* inasmuch as it is for anyone else. To think otherwise would be to think of Heidegger as quite the monster—that Heidegger must consider most human animals as less than human (possibly any one of them other than the *führer* himself). However, this understanding does not follow from Heidegger's texts. It is, instead, founded upon the historical realities of National Socialism as it manifested particularly in Nazi Germany.

No doubt, Gillespie's historical facts ring truer than any theoretical critique which suggest that "*Heidegger's vision of* φρονησις *is fundamentally flawed*". And, while Gillespie's history is elucidating, by the end of the article, we find that he has failed to deliver his initial promise to show that Heidegger's theory of a political economy founded upon *φρονησις* is fundamentally flawed. Therefore, it is clear that Gillespie is a better historian than he is a metaphysician. Insofar as this is the case, we must leave behind Gillespie's interpretation and subsequent critique. But, in doing so, we take from him what was valuable and leave behind what was all-too fashionable in his time.

Martin Heidegger

Nietzsche, Vol 1-2. HarperOne, 1991 and *Nietzsche*, Vol 3-4. HarporOne, 1991. Trans. David Farrell Krell.

By now, I have offered much reflection on Heidegger, both throughout the development of the opuscule and here in this bibliography. And yet, there is still far more that could be said. Therefore, let this bibliography continue to host a fraction of it. Firstly, what should be noted is that the contents of these four volumes on Nietzsche were constructed during the Nazi period of German history, beginning in 1936—this is significant. Evidently, in constructing his lecture course material on Nietzsche's principal concepts, Heidegger had found it necessary to respond to the popular interpretations of Nietzsche and his philosophy. *The blond beast, the overman,* and *will to power* were understood then, as they commonly still are today, as biological, psychological, and/or moral objects. Furthermore, as is well known, such biology and morality had fallen to appropriation by way of Nazi ideologues, including Alfred Baeumler, especially. While this is hardly interesting history today, what we find on display by way of Heidegger's felt political necessity is not only a highly original interpretation of Nietzsche's thought as a whole (including a metaphysical interpretation of Nietzsche's *revenge, will,* and *power*), but also a commitment to thinking purely, "clean", and with discipline. In this case, on display, above all else, is a commitment to thinking about Nietzsche as a metaphysician, whose thought is distinct from anthropology, psychology, biology, and the whole of the mechanical sciences in general. Today, in standing with a bit more distance from the four-volume *Nietzsche,* what strikes me most pronouncedly is just this: the value of such pure and disciplined thinking. Upon first encountering this monk-like self-disciplining, this value stood in stark contrast to the often flattered multidisciplinary and *generalist intellectual* approach—that which is (to be perfectly frank) often found in armchair psychology and sociology. And while there is nothing wrong with the multidisciplinary approach, there can be no denying that it also provides conditions for error by way of muddled thinking. No doubt, there are bad ways of thinking about the world, and bad ways of describing the phenomenal experience. I also understand that those bad ways can pollute the good ways of thinking and describing. Given the uncommonness of such self-discipline in everyday conversation, I give credit to these four volumes for instilling in me the necessary courage to propose a "clean" metaphysics, one that serves as the groundwork needed for considerations on actual economic and political matters.

Martin Heidegger

Parmenides. Indiana University Press, 1998. Trans. Richard Rojcewicz, André Schuwer.

Parmenides collects material taken from a lecture course which Heidegger conducted during the winter term of 1942–1943 at the University of Freiburg. Perhaps most noteworthy is that this volume offers examples of Heidegger's less common practice: polemics. While his criticisms are interjected sparingly, the nature of his narrative is apparent: modernity will fall to critique—not least the method of the industrialized scientist, whose comportment towards the phenomenal experience is not merely interrogation, but described by Heidegger as an "attack" on phenomena. As such, *Parmenides* reads as a historical narrative more than any of Heidegger's other works. Through Heidegger's analysis of Parmenides' didactic poem on the goddess $A\lambda\eta\theta\varepsilon\iota\alpha$, we find a Latinization of Ancient Greek culture, such that truth would later fall into the service of technology within the story of later modernization. What should be noted is that Heidegger's critique of modernity, and of the obscuring of his protagonist, $\alpha\lambda\eta\theta\varepsilon\iota\alpha$, within the commerce of the human animal is still relevant today. We should not forget the crisis of truth in our own time—namely, *post-truth*. For many, this event had signaled the end of democracy outright, insofar as independent news media is a mechanism of technocratic democracy. This failure of democracy and its ripple effects are attested to by the many claims that Trump was inciting an authoritarian regime. Yet, what cannot be overlooked is that this event, and the subsequent problematizing of truth following this event, had provided for a quite peculiar reflection. While perhaps seemingly perverse, it can be argued that post-truth is exactly that which Heidegger sought. Defined by Oxford Languages, post-truth refers to *"relating to or denoting circumstances in which objective facts are less influential in shaping public opinion than appeals to emotion and personal belief"*. Of course, it would be an overstatement to say that Heidegger was interested in devaluing the function of the positive fact (apparently called *"objective facts"* by Oxford) within the commerce of the human animal altogether. All the same, he did wish to ground facts in the more human realm which philosophy is well suited to describe. The lecture course material on Parmenides, therefore, much like several of Heidegger's later compositions, presents the necessity for *a clearing for truth* which cannot be provided for by a scientific "objective" approach. While it is unclear if Heidegger sought intellectual descriptions (truth) as a public phenomenon, or if he merely sought conditions for the human animal to confront truth, it is likely that Heidegger would have seen both the post-truth media frenzy and the Trump presidency as an opportunity.

No matter the case, I would like to close this reflection on Heidegger's *Parmenides* with a personal disclaimer. Despite the universally pejorative application of the term, "post-truth", for myself, I had experienced this media frenzy as an opportunity. This event offered the potential to revisit the very question of the nature of truth—and it offered this possibly on a grand scale. I had hoped to use Heidegger's *Parmenides* for a confrontation with truth during this time, and for an eventual reconstitution of truth within some public body. Unfortunately, that frenzy has come and gone, without any real public confrontation with the nature of truth. This, then, is a quite unfortunate state for truth, to be sure. I can only hope that my opuscule gives reason, once again, to reconsider and reframe "post-truth" as a positive possibility in the future.

Martin Heidegger

Plato's Sophist. Indiana University Press, 1992. Trans. Richard Rojcewicz, André Schuwer.

By now, it must be apparent to my reader that this bibliography has also become something of an autobiography; it has, anyway, provided me with an opportunity for some much-needed autobiographical reflection. Within my story, I can say that *Plato's Sophist* serves as something of a turning point. However, before speaking on this turning point, a few remarks on the content of *Plato's Sophist* are firstly in order. What should be noted is that this volume collects material from Heidegger's lecture course conducted during the winter semester of 1924–1925 at the University of Marburg. As with the four-volume *Nietzsche*, the dates are significant. Heidegger's detailed analysis of Plato's *Sophist* is prepared for by way of an interpretation of Aristotle's *Nicomachean Ethics*. While the analysis of Plato's *Sophist* proves to be highly original (notably, as an exposition on being and non-being), it is only on account of Heidegger's interpretation of Aristotle's *Ethics* that this volume appears in this bibliography. This is because Heidegger's preparatory introduction provides an insight into the process by which Heidegger eventually came to produce the book we know as *Being and Time*, notably constructed during the same period of his life. What is remarkable, then, and particularly to my own story, is that once I had encountered Heidegger's interpretation of Aristotle's *Ethics*, my perspective on Heidegger's *Being and Time* was forever changed. After my encounter, *Being and Time* was, for the first time in my life, displaced from the heavens, so to speak, and planted firmly in the ground of the Western tradition. However, what is more?—this displacement ended something of a nearly ten-year-long godly idolization of Heidegger. "Yes" reading this lecture course material was a turning point for me! After reading Heidegger's interpretation of Aristotle's *Ethics*, Heidegger was, for the first time in my life, *merely* a human. This new-found characterization of Heidegger, then, also served as a pivot. That interpretation provided me with a critical articulation which I have kept with me ever since— namely, the articulation of the anthropocentric bias in the history of Western thought. This began my deviation from the Western philosophical tradition up to and including Heidegger. I later discovered this deviation was not entirely novel. The most popular attestation to this deviation seems to be that which was produced by Derrida, as we find it within the introduction to his *Of Spirit*.

Friedrich Nietzsche

Twilight of the Idols. Penguin, 1990. Trans. Walter Kaufmann, R.J. Hollingdale.

Friedrich Nietzsche: the poet, the philosopher, and the prophet. There is much truth to be found in this tripartite characterization of the German philosopher—particularly, to the characterization of him as a prophet. This is certainly the case if we consider *first economics* philosophy as the philosophy of the metamodern paradigm and of our future economic democracy, as I do. After all, one of the requirements for dwelling within the realm of *first economics* is that one first experiences Nietzsche's prophetic "*twilight of the idols*" and his "*devaluation of the highest values*" in some genuine sense. Of course, to have this experience "genuinely" would mean to experience Nietzsche's nihilism not as a pessimism, but instead as a liberation. Recalling what was discussed in chapter ten of the opuscule, it is only once we have acknowledged our holy rulers as what they are—that is, as tools for domestication—that we can then release ourselves from the domestication projects to which these rulers belong. What must not be overlooked is that Nietzsche's announcement of the twilight already contains within it the reward of such *nihilism as liberation*. His own encounter with the twilight suggests that what follows is a child-like experimentation, as well as a subsequent empowerment in the creation of the world.

Of course, Martin Heidegger also attested to an encounter with the twilight. He described the philosophy lying beyond this event as a reversal of Platonic essentialism and, as such, a reversal of the Western tradition, from Plato up to and including Nietzsche himself. As is well known, this understanding sent Heidegger in search of *the truth of Being*. Yet, what is unclear is if Heidegger understood the twilight as something of a personal event, or as a world-historical event—"*Western nihilism*". This ambiguity regarding the domain of the event of nihilism mirrors that which we find in Heidegger's understanding of *da sein* itself.

Finally, in addition to Nietzsche and Heidegger, I would like to add Ludwig Wittgenstein to the list of thinkers who, frommy vantage point, seem to have genuinely experienced the twilight—at least, in the personal sense. I say this, even if the names *Nietzsche* and *Wittgenstein* are rarely mentioned together in the same sentence. Of course, what should not be overlooked is that each of these three thinkers were led to consider value creation, in one form or another—that is to say, they were led to consider their post-twilight god (whether *Being* or *form of life*) economically. There is a reason why Wittgenstein took up economic examples in one of his later works, entitled *The Brown Book*. Therefore, we can say that Nietzsche, Heidegger, and Wittgenstein are the inceptual philosophers of *first economics* philosophy. Inasmuch, and insofar as I understand the future of democratic governance economically, it should be no surprise to my reader that the construction of my opuscule had also been motivated by a desire to recover these thinkers from the sociological and technological paradigms of thought which have plagued both academic research and colloquial discourse alike, ever since the unimaginable technical power was employed within the political sphere, beginning with WWII. As time goes on, and as the events of WWII become more distant to us, *more historical*, so to speak, I hope that we will soon be disposed for a return to the economical—and this means a return to a time of intellectual thought before Jean-Paul Sartre, Gilles Deleuze, Yuk Hui, *et cetera, et cetera*.

Bonnitta Roy

Open to Participate: *Collective Participatory Process for Emerging Insight.* Alderlore Insight Center, 2014 (unpublished).

Open to Participate was first written as a submission for a chapter in the book *Cohering the Integral We-Space*. Unfortunately, the submission was rejected and, therefore, the report was never published. However, Roy's collected research later landed in my hands, after I had asked Roy for any documentation produced of her experiences with her *Collective Participatory Process for Emerging Insight*. Despite the rejected submission, and the presumed disappointment for Roy, I am quite happy that Roy's report could live on, principally through my own interpretation— at least through the scant selections which I had repeated throughout the opuscule. Of course, much more could be said about Roy's work. However, I must admit that any commentary which I could produce would be quite unsatisfactory. I could not add anything which was not already expressed by Roy, herself—and, no doubt, in better words than I would use. However, because Roy's *Open to Participate* is still unpublished, as of the time of writing this bibliography, and until it is published, I must encourage my reader to consider Roy's other works, alongside the opuscule. Notable is her two-part article series, *Tale of Two Systems*, published to Emerge.com. I would like to emphasize Roy's critique of "*the social imaginary*" as it appears in this series. This critique echoes my own concern regarding an overly sociological outlook on the phenomenal experience. Then, in the second part of this series, Roy promotes a "*digital naturalism*". I understand this form of naturalism not simply as a return to Auguste Comte's positivism, but, instead, as one way in which we could return our attention to the phenomenal experience, yet also away from any priority which the human animal currently enjoys within the socio-logical and technological "worldviews". In addition to this series, I recommend Roy's six-part series on *reducing complexity*—published to her Medium.com page. Also worthy of mention are Roy's expositions on *neo-animism*. As the name suggests, neo-animism animates our pagan heritage. Roy's expositions on neo-animism are archived on her Sub-stack.com newsletter, The Pop-Up School.

Bertie Russell

Beyond the Local Trap: New Municipalism and the Rise of the Fearless Cities. Antipode, 2019.

Bertie Russell's *Beyond the Local Trap: New Municipalism and the Rise of the Fearless Cities* stands in a similar place as *Shifting Baselines of Europe* within this bibliography. Both publications provided me with invaluable quotes from various representatives of the municipalist movement. I am quite indebted to both of these publications in that regard. However, having said that, perhaps Russell's section titled *The Feminization of Politics*, in particular, demands further reflection. What should be obvious to anyone who has read this section is that the character of this "*feminization*" is epistemological, and, to be sure, this feminization does, in part, belong to the liberal project. Russell explicitly says that, "*The most visible aspect of the 'feminization of politics' is ensuring that women play a prominent role throughout leadership and representative positions*". Of course, from a post-liberal position, this "*visibility*" strikes us as archaic. And, to be honest, it does feel as though Russell is pandering to those resonating with Left-leaning narratives. However, not to be mistaken, this *"visibility"* does not exhaust the value of such a "feminization". And, after all, what we find upon deeper inspection is that such optics are grounded upon a much more profound and novel political activity. I will repeat again from an anonymous contributor of Argentina's Ciudad Futura,

> "[The feminization of politics] managed to turn the conversation about feminism around, about the need for a society of equals where the struggle isn't anchored in the liberal, from the point of view of individual rights. Rather, it's the opposite, the idea of a model for society."

And from Russell, herself, we read that,

> "The feminization of politics speaks to a shift away from a politics of separation—*they* govern, from afar, alienated from the everyday—towards the politics of proximity—*we* govern, in a close way, connected to the experience of the everyday. It is fundamentally a radical democratic concept, one that puts a focus on transforming *how* decision-making takes place, who has a right to speak, and how we engage with one another."

It could be said that the successes of the municipalist movement signal a potential transformation of modernity's *grand politics*. They also help us to picture for ourselves a future where politicians might stand beside their public, on social media and in public gatherings, for example; but not above them, as we find animate in technocratic forms of democracy. Therefore, for my part, I say let us join in this so-called *"feminization of politics"*—but in doing so, let us find a new name. We must leave behind the metaphysics of individual-subjectivity and those arguments which are produced from the liberal position. No doubt, in doing so, we will have manifested a maturity which is indicative of the post-liberal position.

E.F. Schumacher

Small is Beautiful. Vintage, 1993. (Originally published in 1973).

The legacy of E.F. Schumacher's *Small is Beautiful* is well known. Inspiring activist movements such as Buy Locally and Fair Trade, this book was an essential piece of early Green Movement literature during the 1970s. However, while its legacy is often cited (along with its relevance in future political activism), unfortunately, this *applicative* type of talk has overshadowed talk of the book's metaphysics. And yet, Schumacher was particularly concerned with the message that metaphysics had to offer. To be sure, we only need to consider the fact that the word *metaphysics* appears throughout *Small is Beautiful* a surprising number of times, especially after considering that it is a collection of reflections on economics and includes only economic prescriptions. Note that Schumacher's affinity for locale, labor, and communion, also suggests that he was familiar with Martin Heidegger's metaphysics, or possibly that these two thinkers were inspired by similar intellectual traditions. However, at the time of writing this bibliography, I must admit that I have only a shallow understanding of Schumacher's biography, and therefore, I am not confident to say much on Schumacher's understanding of the relationship between metaphysics and economics, outside of what is presented in *Small is Beautiful*. Specifically, I have no idea if he was acquainted with Heidegger's expositions. (Note that it is almost certain that he was familiar with Ludwig Wittgenstein.) Despite this, I am sure of one thing: in taking up economics as the applicable domain for his metaphysics, Schumacher is deanimating solutions of other forms. Specifically, he is not championing for: 1) self-help solutions founded upon the disciplines of psychology or upon Western spirituality (Schumacher seems to have understood, as I do, that solutions making use of a Christian church which has been utterly liberated from commercial activity would only pacify the population, in order that the population may suffer peacefully from within their economic conditions); 2) nor is Schumacher championing self-help solutions, such as those found within the imported practices of Eastern mysticism, which, again, pulls the human animal away from everyday commerce in order that he may suffer from within it; 3) nor does Schumacher champion for social conditioning and a domestication of the human animal—or some other project founded upon some other form of sociologic; 4) nor is he interested in rights or the laws which protect those rights, whether those laws are policed by administrative governance or by social governance. Instead, Schumacher, much like Heidegger, is interested in the robustness of *everyday commerce*; he turned towards economic solutions. This is not to be shunted aside. And because of this, he is a premier economist to be considered in the application of metaphysical description to material economics. And so, while a comparison may be awkward, we can place E.F. Schumacher, the economist, in the void which was left in denouncing Aleksandr Dugin, the anthropologist, as one possible successor to Heidegger's early metaphysics.

Ludwig Wittgenstein

Zettel. University of California Press, 1967. Trans. G.E.M. Anscombe.

Unfortunately, the development of the opuscule did not provide an opportunity to say more on the philosophy of Ludwig Wittgenstein. But, to be sure, all that could be said, was said. Despite this, I do feel a personal reflection might be in order; after all, I am compelled to do justice to the influence which Wittgenstein's writings have had on my own life. But first, let me share a few remarks on Wittgenstein's biography, then I will use those remarks to reflect on my own life story.

As for Wittgenstein, what should be noted is that he was writing in the first half of the twentieth century. He seems to have been responding to the major scientific advances of his time. In fact, he was quite critical of the pursuit of the scientific industries and of their ability to uncover the ultimate truths about reality. In one of his notes collected and published posthumously in the book *Culture and Value*, we read his lament that, *"It is all one to me whether or not the typical Western scientist understands or appreciates my work, since he will not in any case understand the spirit in which I write".* Of course, for those of us having grown up in the United States during the 1990s, we remember that physics had then served as the explain-all science of the time. Richard Dawkins, Sam Harris, and Neil DeGrasse Tyson enjoyed celebrity during this decade—likely because they took part in a quite polarized debate, with science on one side and religion on the other. Having been impressed by this debate early in my adult life, I found myself wanting to answer the apparent discordance between religion and science on my own terms, later in my adult life. And, to be honest, even as

I compose this bibliography, I still feel the pain of when the American people were critiqued for their "anti-intellectualism" and for their "anti-scientism". Of course, as is likely no surprise, I found my answers within Western philosophy. Wittgenstein's writings and, in particular, the notebook clippings collected and published as *Zettel*, had proven invaluable in my pursuits. Of the various notes, I spent the most time with his phenomenological studies. I understand that phenomenology is quite well suited for placing scientific descriptions and explanations (and, especially, those provided by physics) within the whole of the phenomenal experience. The same can be said for the descriptions and explanations provided by Christianity. However, and in addition to this, *Zettel* also presents Wittgenstein's best style; rather than adopting the overly burdened language of the Western philosophical tradition, he uses ordinary language to approach philosophical elucidation. Therefore, Wittgenstein's style welcomes a space for the activity of philosophizing. For me, this *activity* has always stood in stark contrast to the *passivity* of product consumption, spectator sports, and "yes", the mere repetition of historical texts (Christianity) and the digestion of scientific knowledge.

Later in my life, when I found myself partnering with the historical and cultural center, Spinderihallerne, in Vejle, Denmark, and when facilitating the International Salons on Philosophy, Wittgenstein's phenomenological studies continued to provide value to my life and, therefore, to others by extension. Perhaps I would say that for me (and quite contrary to Wittgenstein) it does matter if, whether or not, the typical Western scientist understands the spirit of Wittgenstein's works. Considering all that had been said throughout my opuscule, it should be clear that for me, in order to save democracy as a form of governance in which truth matters to the human animal, Wittgenstein's philosophical elucidations are of paramount importance.

Glossary of Key Terms

While the format of this glossary will be familiar to you in many respects, it will also be unfamiliar in others. Therefore, I feel that it requires a proper introduction. In addition to serving as a reference for novel or specialized words used throughout the opuscule, this glossary will also serve as a summary of the key terms used in the metaphysical architectonic constructed over the course of the opuscule. Many terms within this summary require an explanation first before others can be introduced. Therefore, I have chosen to let the architectonic's narrative decide the order in which the terms should be listed. This means that this glossary will *not* be ordered alphabetically, as is the standard practice. Additionally, it should be said that this glossary is not meant to be comprehensive. Specifically, it does not include every foreign word which was used throughout the opuscule. However, most of the Ancient Greek, Latin, and Anglo-Saxon words appearing throughout the development have also been followed by their respective parenthetical pronunciations and translations. Therefore, unless a foreign word is relevant to the summary of the metaphysical architectonic, then it will not be featured here. Furthermore, I have chosen to divide the summary's narrative into three divisions: *discipline*, *nature*, and *politics*. These labels are not meant to further qualify the terms, say, categorically. Rather, I have merely taken some artistic liberties in framing the narrative of the summary. While I could have opted for a more traditional glossary, I hope that my reader agrees with my choice to print a combined glossary/summary on these pages.

DISCIPLINE

metaphysics, from Aristotle's τα μετα τα φυσικα ("the [writings] after the Physics"). Today, the word *metaphysics* can refer to at least two categories of description. The first category refers to objects which fall outside the possibility of physical description, yet are in a causal relationship with the objects of the physical world. This type can be exemplified by objects such as *luck*, *power*, and *will*. The second category refers to those objects which belong to a description of the conditions for experience, or the conditions for the world *to be*. Two philosophers are regarded as the premier metaphysicians of the modern era, namely Immanuel Kant and Martin Heidegger. Kant sought a description of the conditions for experience—"internal" time and "external" space, for example. Heidegger sought the conditions for the world *to be*. While both meanings of metaphysics have been used throughout the opuscule, those objects which belong to the first category have been designated as *causal-occult*, while the second category require no extra qualification.

subject, from Latin *subicio*, a compound of Latin *sub* ("under, beneath, at the foot of") and *iacio* ("I lay, set, establish, build, found, construct"). Within scientific disciplines, various objects serve as subject matter, such that all discourse within that discipline is directed towards those grounding subjects. For example, *man* in the case of anthropology; *the psyche* in the case of psychology; or *society* in the case of sociology. Within the philosophy of *first economics*, the subject is the subject matter of economic reform; and, at the same time, it is also the object of a metaphysical architectonic. As such an object, the subject (namely, discourse) is also the condition for experience (Kant), and the condition for the world *to be* (Heidegger)—or, in the language of *first economics* philosophy, it is the condition for value creation.

discourse, as the subject of *first economics*, discourse refers to the primordial ground which cannot be expressed in description. As the condition for values, it is pre-linguistic and pre-cognitive. Being such a condition, discourse is metaphysical.

***first economics* philosophy**, named in accordance with Aristotle's τα περι της πρωτης φιλοσοφιας ("the [writings] concerning first philosophy"). *First economics* is a discipline concerned with the description of the conditions for value creation. It takes as its subject matter our primordial *wheeling and dealing within nature*—discourse. Within *first economics* philosophy, every object, whether *food* and *chair*, or *feminism* and *liberty* (or even those objects of "subjective" experience, *grief*, *hope*, or *love*, for example), are treated as *values*. Their existence is dependent on their having value to living, and, as such, are themselves constituted in being a value. Insofar as the world presents itself from within the "radius" which is the πολις (*polis*), *first economics* is essentially political in nature.

phenomenological commitment, refers to a commitment to phenomena, as they appear of themselves, as the objects which they are. This commitment presupposes an understanding that any object is nothing other than what it presents itself as. Whether we are speaking of a smartphone or of a person's soul, these objects are phenomena that can be traced to a phenomenological experience. This commitment is not so much part of the metaphysical architectonic of *first economics*; rather, it is a virtue for maintaining within this domain of thought.

NATURE

λογος (*logos*), an Ancient Greek word which has been translated into Modern English variously as *speech, oration, discourse, quote, story, study, ratio, word, calculation,* and *reason*. Therefore, we must conclude that *λογος* can only be understood from within the text in which we find it. In Aristotle's writing, for example, *λογος* is equivalent to "the word" (as in, for example, "In the beginning, there was the word".) From the fragments which have been ascribed to Heraclitus, *λογος* seems to have referred to an object. "*All things come to be in accordance with logos.*" First economics begins its understanding with this fragment. *Λογος* is that by which phenomena come into accord with one another.

καθολου (*katholou*), an Ancient Greek word which translates into Modern English as "universal" or "the whole". In *first economics*, *καθολου* describes the essence of *λογος*.

καθ εκαστον (*kath hēkaston*), an Ancient Greek word which translates into Modern English as "the particular" or "the particulars". Therefore, this term is complementary to καθολου. In *first economics*, we can think of καθ εκαστον as "the actuals". It refers to that which is articulated, defined, and, in some cases, described by way of the καθολου of λογος.

actio, from Latin, meaning "act of doing or making". In *first economics* philosophy, *actio* refers to any primordial "action" which presences the world. In the first half of the opuscule, επιστημη was characterized as an "apprehension" of the phenomenal experience. It serves as an example of such a primordial "action". The second half of the opuscule offers αληθευειν (*alētheuein*) as an alternative.

ομοιωσις (*homoiosis*), in *first economics* philosophy, ομοιωσις refers to an "event" of "making like". We can imagine this event by way of the so-called "theory of forms" and Plato's ιδεα (*idea*). Taking the example of a chair, we would say that ομοιωσις presences the ιδεα "chair" (καθολου) as the particular chair that it is (καθ εκαστον). Ομοιωσις is ecstatic. Either the phenomenon presents itself as what it is, or it presents itself in the form of a guise, or ψευδης (*pseudōs*). Ομοιωσις is equally natural—that is to say, there is no individual-subject mediating ομοιωσις. In modern language, we would say that the event of ομοιωσις takes place in the "objective" domain—this event is external to any individual.

nature, in *first economics* philosophy, nature refers to the way of being of phenomena. That which is natural shows itself, as it is, of itself.

αληθευειν (*alētheuein*), from Ancient Greek. In Aristotle's writing, αληθευειν refers to a way of human being. In Modern Greek, we might express Aristotle's αληθευειν as "to truth" (as in, for example, "to walk"). Αληθευειν is a way of *being towards the truth*, so to speak. In Modern English, we might express αληθευειν as "sincerity", "honesty", or "genuineness". In the architectonic of *first economics* philosophy, αληθευειν refers to the *actio* of adherence; specifically, the adherence of the object as a constant ομοιωσις. That is to say, αληθευειν refers to the way of being of natural phenomena which adhere as true. We might say that αληθευειν is not a personal "subjective" way to be (either sincere or genuine), but is instead a genuineness of the "objective" world in being what it is.

POLITICS

ποιησις (*poiēsis*), an Ancient Greek word which translates into Modern English as "creation" or "production". *Ποιησις* derives from the Ancient Greek ποιεω (*poieō*, "I make"). Note that the Modern English words *poet, poetry,* and *poetic* also derive from ποιεω. In *first economics,* the artistic character of ποιησις is preserved.

δημιουργος (*dēmiurgos*), an Ancient Greek word which translates into Modern English as "the creator" or "craftsman". In Platonic thought, δημιουργος refers to the way of being as a craftsman who produces the ιδεα of the δημος (*dēmos*)—that is to say, the δημιουργος produces the outward appearance of the world within the commerce of public uses of things and of communal life. In *first economics* philosophy, δημιουργος refers to the way of being engaged within the "radius" which is the πολις. It is the way of being civically engaged.

δημος (*dēmos*), an Ancient Greek word which translates into Modern English as "the public" or "the people". We can think of δημος as καθολου—as a universal *any one of us.* At the same time, the δημος is the *"We, the people"* who is *a no one in particular*. In *Being and Time*, Heidegger argues that having a preliminary understanding of the δημος is necessary for any particular one of us (any objectified *you* or a *me*), to be articulated as the actual one who they are. When operating within *first economics* philosophy, we can extend that oneness between the δημιουργος and the δημος to all of nature.

πολις (*polis*), an Ancient Greek word which translates into Modern English as "the city" or "one's community". In *first economics*, the πολις refers to the "radius" of discourse in nature and together with the natural. At the epicenter of the radius, we find the locus of creation and authenticity. This locus is itself temporal, insofar as that locus is equally the moment of *the encounter*. The primordial "action" at this moment produces articulation; it produces definition and, in some cases, description. Therefore, within the metaphysical architectonic of *first economics*, the πολις is the "forum" of truth. Projection (or simply, *the project*) is the essence of the πολις, insofar as discourse is itself grounded upon projection.

αληθεια (*alētheia*), an Ancient Greek word which has traditionally been translated into Modern English as "truth". However, when looking at the word's construction, αληθεια literally reads as "unforgetfulness". And while both of these translations are still in use today, Martin Heidegger's interpretation of αληθεια as "unconcealedness" has not been forgotten. Both *unforgetfulness* and *unconcealedness* equally preserve the privative alpha and the word's construction: α + ληθη (*lēthē*, "oblivion, forgetfulness, concealment") + ια. It should be noted that the architectonic of *first economics* does not explicitly make use of this word.

truth, in *first economics* philosophy, truth refers to the description which adheres ($\alpha\lambda\eta\theta\varepsilon\upsilon\varepsilon\iota\nu$) as true in the moment of *the encounter*. Truth is therefore, disclosive of the phenomenal experience. However, truth is likewise projective. Insofar as this is the case, only together, in each moment, in the very forum at the encounter, can the truth be revealed as the truth which has always been and which could never have been otherwise. In being both disclosive and projective, truth can be produced from the mouth of a human animal, or it can be produced from phenomena altogether besides this animal. As an example, when we say that the ruler *says* "five inches", then the ruler "speaks" the truth. Therefore, this truth, like all others, whether from the mouth of a human animal, a non-human animal, or a machine, marks the epicenter of the "radius", the $\pi o\lambda\iota\varsigma$, where we find the locus of creation and authenticity.

$\kappa o\iota\nu\omega\nu\iota\alpha$ (*koinonia*), an Ancient Greek word which translates into Modern English as either a "joint participation", or "a share which anyone has in anything". We can also think of $\kappa o\iota\nu\omega\nu\iota\alpha$ as a fellowship or communion; and inasmuch, it is equivalent to Latin *societas*. In *first economics* philosophy, $\kappa o\iota\nu\omega\nu\iota\alpha$ refers to the being of that which is participating in the producing or presencing of the world.

About the Author

Justin Carmien grew up in Northern Indiana. On his father's side of the family, his great-grandfather, John Raber, ran for the congressional office of Indiana's second district. After losing to Charles Helleck, the incumbent Republican leader of the House of Representatives in 1964, Justin's great-grandfather established Raber Golf, an eighteen-hole golf course located just outside the village of Bristol, Indiana. This business has remained under his family's operation up until today.

In his own adult life, Justin first entered the workforce as an entrepreneur. After establishing a publishing company in the United States, he later moved to Denmark in order to further pursue a career in product design and marketing. During his later years in Denmark, Justin partnered with Spinderihallerne, a municipality-run community and historical center located in the provincial town of Vejle. During this partnership, Justin worked closely with international community developers to host salons on philosophy. Then, in 2017, Justin founded a YouTube channel. Justin's channel received acclaim for his videos sharing reflections on Scandinavian political philosophy, and, in particular, his own experiences within the metamodern political movement.

Today, Justin continues to add novel contributions to the metamodern movement by drawing from the tradition of metaphysics—including his reading of metaphysics as a *primordial economics*. Justin's own *first economics* philosophy follows from the German philosopher Martin Heidegger's interpretation of Aristotle's *Metaphysics*, as well as Heidegger's interpretation of Friedrich Nietzsche as a value metaphysician. Through *first economics* philosophy, Justin teaches a metaphysics of value creation—a metaphysics which not only describes the "artist phenomenon" of the craftsman, but is also, in his own words, "*equally that of the πολιτικος, the politician*". *First economics* philosophy promises the discipline of metaphysics as a political answer. This book, *How to Nurture Truth and Authenticity*, marks a milestone in the development of this philosophy.

Milton Keynes UK
Ingram Content Group UK Ltd.
UKHW040627310723
426074UK00001B/84